ROBERT NISBET

LIBRARY OF MODERN THINKERS

EDITED BY JEFFREY O. NELSON

ROBERT NISBET
BY BRAD LOWELL STONE

ERIC VOEGELIN
BY MICHAEL P. FEDERICI *(Forthcoming)*

MICHAEL OAKESHOTT
BY TIMOTHY FULLER *(Forthcoming)*

LUDWIG VON MISES
BY ISRAEL KIRZNER *(Forthcoming)*

WILHELM RÖPKE
BY JOHN ZMIRAK *(Forthcoming)*

FRANCIS GRAHAM WILSON
BY H. LEE CHEEK *(Forthcoming)*

BERTRAND DE JOUVENEL
BY DANIEL MAHONEY *(Forthcoming)*

ANDREW LYTLE
BY MARK MALVASI *(Forthcoming)*

WILL HERBERG
BY VIGEN GUROIAN *(Forthcoming)*

ROBERT NISBET

COMMUNITARIAN TRADITIONALIST

Brad Lowell Stone

OGLETHORPE UNIVERSITY

ISI BOOKS
WILMINGTON, DELAWARE
2000

The Library of Modern Thinkers is published in cooperation with Collegiate Network, Inc. Generous grants from the Sarah Scaife Foundation, Earhart Foundation, F. M. Kirby Foundation, Castle Rock Foundation, Wilbur Foundation, and the William H. Donner Foundation made this series possible. The Intercollegiate Studies Institute and Collegiate Network, Inc., gratefully acknowledge their support.

Cataloging-in-Publication Data

Stone, Brad Lowell.
      Robert Nisbet : communitarian
      traditionalist / by Brad Lowell Stone.—
      1st ed.—Wilmington, Del. : ISI Books, 2000.

      p. ; cm.

      ISBN 1-882926-48-X
      1. Nisbet, Robert A. 2. Conservatism. I. Title.

JC573 .S76 2000   00-1011146
320.5/2—dc21   CIP

Published in the United States by:

    ISI Books
    In cooperation with Collegiate Network, Inc.
    Post Office Box 4431
    Wilmington, DE 19807-0431

Cover and interior design by Sam Torode

Printed in Canada

CONTENTS

ACKNOWLEDGMENTS

IF ACKNOWLEDGMENTS are a means for paying intellectual debts I must commence by acknowledging my gratitude to Dr. Manning Pattillo and Oglethorpe University. I was appointed at Oglethorpe in 1982 when Dr. Pattillo was serving as president. Before interviewing anyone for the position, Manning consulted with Robert Nisbet (whom I met just once, a year later). Dr. Nisbet told Manning that no fresh Ph.D. in sociology was likely to be anything more than a needle-nosed specialist and that the best Manning could hope for was someone who displayed some small sign that he or she might grow in the job once hired. Whatever I said in the interview that secured the offer had to have been very small and quite feeble indeed. I am very grateful to Dr. Pattillo and to Oglethorpe for my appointment and for providing one of the most stimulating and intellectually liberating environments imaginable. At

Oglethorpe, I benefit daily from my friendships with Alan Woolfolk, Bill Shropshire, John Orme, Joseph Knippenberg, Monte Wolf, and Mike Rulison.

I am also grateful to Bruce Frohnen, George Carey, and Peter Lawler for invitations to two 1996 conferences that stimulated my interest in communitarianism. Bruce and George invited me to participate in a Liberty Fund colloquium on "Liberty and Community," and Peter was the person most responsible for organizing the Berry College conference on "Communitarianism and Civil Society." I gained a great deal from each of these gatherings and I am very thankful for the invitations to participate.

In preparing this book I was helped tremendously by comments on the whole manuscript by Jeff Nelson, Christopher Briggs, Alan Woolfolk, and an anonymous reviewer. Jeff's comments improved every chapter but were especially helpful in improving chapter 2, and Chris and Alan provided needed help when I was deciding the form of the final chapter. I am very grateful to each of these men and to the anonymous reviewer.

Small portions of the introduction first appeared in "A True Sociologist: Robert Nisbet" in *The Intercollegiate Review* (Spring 1998):38-42. The final chapter draws from two previously published essays: "Classical Liberalism and Sociology" in *Sociological Forum* (Fall 1997): 497-512; and "Statist Communitarianism and

Civil Society" in *The Intercollegiate Review* (Spring 1997): 9-18. I am grateful to Plenum Publishers and to the Intercollegiate Studies Institute for permission to use these materials here.

Finally, my largest debt of gratitude is to my wife, Becky, and to my children, Katie and Robert. They make everything worthwhile. This book and my life are dedicated to them.

ABBREVIATIONS AND
REFERENCES

ALL PAGE REFERENCES in the text are to Nisbet's writings. When referring to his books, I use the following abbreviations, and when referring to his other writings, I use the years of publication as identified below. All other references are in the endnotes.

Books

QC *The Quest for Community: A Study in the Ethics of Order and Freedom* (New York: Oxford University Press, 1953). Reprinted in 1962 and 1970 by Oxford and in 1990 by the Institute for Contemporary Studies Press.

DAD *The Degradation of Academic Dogma: The University in America, 1945-1970* (New York: Basic Books, 1971). Re-published by Transaction Press, 1996.

MMS *The Making of Modern Society* (New York: NYU Press, 1986).

SB   *The Social Bond: An Introduction to the Study of Society* (New York: Knopf, 1970).

TS   *Teachers and Scholars: A Memoir of Berkeley in Depression and War* (New Brunswick, N.J.: Transaction Press, 1992).

ST   *The Sociological Tradition* (New York: Basic Books, 1966). Republished by Transaction Press, 1993.

HIP   *History of the Idea of Progress* (New York: Basic Books, 1980). Republished by Transaction Press, 1993.

C   *Conservatism: Dream and Reality* (Minneapolis: University of Minnesota Press, 1986).

P   *Prejudices: A Philosophical Dictionary* (Cambridge, Mass.: Harvard University Press, 1982).

SED   *The Sociology of Emile Durkheim* (New York: Oxford University Press, 1974).

PA   *The Present Age: Progress and Anarchy in Modern America* (New York: Harper and Row, 1988).

SAF   *Sociology as an Art Form* (New York: Oxford University Press, 1976).

SP   *The Social Philosophers: Community and Conflict in Western Thought* (New York: Washington Square Press, 1982). First published by Crowell, 1973.

TR   *Tradition and Revolt: Historical and Sociological Essays* (New York: Random House, 1968). Republished by Transaction Press, 1999.

SCH   *Social Change and History* (New York: Oxford University Press, 1969).

TA   *Twilight of Authority* (New York: Oxford University Press, 1975). A new edition, with a foreword by Robert G. Perrin, was republished by Liberty Press, 2000.

RS   *Roosevelt and Stalin: The Failed Courtship* (Washington, D.C.: Regnery Gateway, 1988).

Other Writings

1943   "The French Revolution and the Rise of Sociology in France," *The American Journal of Sociology*, 49 (November 1943), 156-164.

1952   "Conservatism and Sociology," *The American Journal of Sociology*, 48 (September 1952), 167-175.

1962   "Preface to the Galaxy Edition," in *Community and Power* (from the 1962 paperback edition of *The Quest for Community*).

1974   "The Decline of Academic Nationalism," *Change*, 6 (July/August 1974), 26-31.

1986   "Foreword" to *The American Family and the State*, edited by Joseph R. Peden and Fred Glahe (San Francisco: Pacific Research Institute, 1986), xix-xxvi.

INTRODUCTION

HENRI BERGSON ONCE OBSERVED that a truly great thinker says just one thing in his life because he has only one point of contact with the real. By this Bergson meant that although a great thinker might have a variety of interests, he typically embraces one great truth that animates each of his pursuits and serves as a guide to lesser truths. Whether or not this holds true generally, it is true of Robert Nisbet, the subject of this study. In virtually every one of his eighteen books, and in the majority of his numerous articles, Professor Nisbet asserts that the twentieth century's preoccupation with community is a result of the erosion of intermediate communities—family, neighborhood, religious association, and voluntary association—caused by the structure and activities of the Western political state. In his works, of course, he emphasizes different components of this theme—the nature of genuine community, the conditions of liberty, the contexts fostering individuality, the intellectual sources of statism, and the intellectual Remnant advocating social pluralism. Still, whether the topic is the degradation of academic dogma, the "alienation" of postwar Americans, the crisis in Western authority, or the history of sociological theory, the overarching theme never changes.

Nisbet first announced his grand theme in *The Quest for Community*. The book was published in 1953 at the end of a three-year period that produced what Nisbet calls a "freshet of books" with an unmistakable conservative character: Russell Kirk's *The Conservative Mind*, Eric Voegelin's *The New Science of Politics*, William Buckley's *God and Man at Yale*, and Daniel Boorstin's *The Genius of American Politics*. The year 1953, Russell Kirk observed, was "the year the liberals began to listen," and, although Kirk's book was probably most responsible for this, reviewers all across the political spectrum gave Nisbet's *Quest* wide and warm attention. But the book's influence has gone well beyond its initial impact. The book has been through four editions (most recently, the Institute of Contemporary Studies' 1990 edition) and has been in print for most of the last half century. This is because, in many respects, the book has gained pertinence over time. Although initially it was read most fervently by conservative readers, it influenced certain New Left writers in the 1960s, and, moreover, it swayed the rhetoric and style of American conservatism in the 1970s and 1980s so much so that Nicholas

Lemann wrote in 1991 of "the triumph of Nisbetism as the stated creed of American politics at the highest level."

Lemann overstates the case, but Nisbet nevertheless anticipated by almost a half century what is currently being said by numerous academics, public intellectuals, and politicians of every political stripe who rhapsodize over the virtues of community and bemoan their decline. Yet, we should not forget that certain "communitarians" (such as Michael Sandel, Alan Ehrenhalt, and Amitai Etzioni) and "civil society" theorists (such as Don Eberly, Francis Fukuyama, Robert Putnum, Peter Berger, and Richard John Neuhaus) are often simply echoing ideas first expressed long ago by Nisbet and which he developed extensively over the course of his very productive career.[3]

Although in the final chapter of this study I am analytical and, on one point, critical, my chief aim here is to draw attention to Nisbet's prescient and truly insightful thought by presenting a close and clear exposition of his work. This study is offered to any interested reader, but readers of the generation that has come of age as many of Nisbet's books have gone out of print could find it especially useful. Regarding the book's organization, because Nisbet was so consistent in his thinking I do not need to explicate his work, book by book. My approach is thematic. In successive chapters, I analyze the separate threads that form Nisbet's grand theme. In several chapters, I draw from a dozen or so of his books in developing a single topic.

Specifically, in chapter 1, I briefly describe the main events of Nisbet's life. In chapter 2, I describe Nisbet's social history of the eclipse of community by state power and discuss the consequences for the individual. Chapter 3 treats Nisbet's characterization of the ideas that have both shaped and reflected the concrete changes in community and state power in the modern era. In it I reconstruct Nisbet's portraits of two traditions in Western social and political philosophy: political monism and social pluralism. Chapter 4 surveys Nisbet's various writings on conservatism as both an intellectual and social movement, with special emphasis on what Nisbet calls "conservative dogmatics"—the coherent, persistent, almost sacred beliefs that determine the lives of conservatives. Chapter 5 examines Nisbet's reflections on the two fields in which he taught and wrote: sociology and history. I describe his view of the emergence of sociology out of the conservative reaction to the French Revolution, his writings on sociology as an art form, and his analysis of developmentalism in historical accounts of social change. In the sixth and final chapter I make an assessment of Nisbet's work and appraise his legacy. Somewhat critically, I suggest that by paying little attention to certain classical liberals, Nisbet overlooked important intellectual backing for his defense of social pluralism and for his forays against political monism. The bulk of this chapter, however, is a comparison between Nisbet's pluralistic communitarianism and Robert Bellah's monistic or statist communitarianism. I explore the comparison because although many "communitarians," including those mentioned above, often reiterate arguments made by Nisbet, Bellah represents a type of contemporary communitarian who confuses community with state power—a fateful and very dangerous confusion, according to Nisbet. Since the weight of empirical evidence is on Nisbet's, not Bellah's, side, I conclude that Nisbet is the vastly superior guide to the present age.

LIFE

ROBERT NISBET WAS BORN in Los Angeles, California, on September 30, 1913, but he never lived there. His parents loathed the small desert town of Maricopa, where they lived, and as Nisbet reports in *Teachers and Scholars*, his "mother was bound, and my loving father therefore was too, that she would not have her first born in such topographical and squalid circumstances, that she would go the hundred miles or so required to reach Los Angeles and deliver her first amid civilized people and folkways" (TS, 2). Because of his father's work, the family returned immediately to Maricopa after Robert's birth. This oil town in the desert, Nisbet says, proved to be a blessing because its ugliness drove him "straight to books for haven and experience of the vicarious."

When he was five years old, Robert, his two-year-old brother, and his parents moved to Macon, Georgia, his father's birthplace and the place where his paternal grandparents lived. While in Macon, Robert's mother gave birth to her third son, almost dying in the process. She was pregnant with twins, one of whom died in birth. She delivered at home partly because she was a Christian Scientist and would not go to a hospital (Nisbet's father was Presbyterian but assented to her wishes). This too, Nisbet says, may have been a blessing in disguise. "Antisepsis was only just becoming known in a great many places at the time, and there were surely more deaths than lives saved in the vast majority of hospitals in 1918" (TS, 3).

Robert began school in Macon, and although the family was there just two years, they were important two years. He reports that it was long after the family returned to California "before I got over the feeling, the very strong feeling, that I was a Southerner." Many years later, when he was at the University of California, Berkeley, he read the Southern Agrarian mani-festo *I'll Take My Stand*. He says, "the quickness with which I found myself agreeing with most of it was probably sufficient evidence that my road to political conservatism began with a considerable dosage of Southern Conservatism, the result of a couple of years in Macon" (TS, 6).

When the family returned to California it settled again in Maricopa, where Robert's father managed a lumberyard. "Education," Nisbet says, "was supreme among the lares and penates of our hearth." Along with the excellence of California public schools, education was the constant in the life of the Nisbet family as they moved to Santa Cruz when Robert was in the sixth grade and then two years later to San Luis Obispo where he spent his high school years.

In 1932 Nisbet enrolled at Berkeley. With the exception of the period between 1943-1946, when he served in the army, he remained there for the next twenty-one years, first as an undergraduate, then as a graduate student, and, finally, as a faculty member. According to his own accounts, his Berkeley years were remarkable. Among the many excellent scholars that crossed Nisbet's path as an undergraduate, he was most impressed by the unorthodox cultural historian Frederick J. Teggart. Nisbet says he was "smitten" by Teggart, a man who "was almost evangelical when he was describing, say, the advantages of comparative history over orthodox, unilinear, narrative history or, in a different tenor, the built-in conflict between family and state in the history of humankind" (MMS, 6). So impressed was the young Nisbet by Teggart that when he completed his undergraduate studies he decided to pursue his Ph.D. under Teggart's direction in the Department of Social Institutions—a department created by the university to accommodate Teggart's fractious genius. He became Teggart's teaching assistant for a year-long course titled Progress and Civilization, the very course in which Nisbet was smitten as an undergraduate by Teggart.

While in graduate school, Nisbet attended Max Radin's

course in Roman law, which sustained and supplemented Teggart's observations concerning the perpetual tension between intermediate social groups and the state, and he immersed himself in Otto von Gierke's study of intermediate association in the Middle Ages. He completed his graduate work in just three years. His dissertation, published as *Social Group and French Thought* by Arno Press in 1980, was on the "Reactionary Enlightenment," chiefly the thinking of Bonald, de Maistre, Lamennais, and Chateaubriand.

After completing his Ph.D. in 1939, he was appointed an instructor in the Department of Social Institutions. In 1942 he was promoted to assistant professor and got his first taste of academic administration while serving as assistant dean of the College of Letters and Science until he enlisted in the army in 1943. He enlisted for a variety of reasons, including his unhappiness with the militarization and bureaucratization of the wartime Berkeley campus and a promise by an enlistment sergeant that, because he was volunteering, he could have his choice of war theaters. The thought of seeing Europe for the first time was "a wonderful stimulant" to enlisting, but, alas, the sergeant lied, and Nisbet spent two years in the Pacific theater, chiefly on Oahu and Saipan.

He returned to Berkeley in early 1946. Teggart had retired in 1940, so the administration changed the name of the department to which Nisbet returned by adding "Sociology." The period between 1946 and 1953 was busy for Nisbet but also fecund. He studied the works of the so-called British pluralists—F. W. Maitland, Ernest Barker (both of whom translated von Gierke), J. N. Figgis, and the young Harold Laski—and for the first time probed the works of his two greatest intellectual heroes, Edmund Burke and Alexis de Tocqueville, whose rediscovery in American thought, Nisbet reports, "started to really flower" in the late forties and early fifties. During this period Nisbet had a full teaching load, served on many university committees, and wrote his first book, *The Quest for Community: A Study in the Ethics of Order and Freedom.* His work was rewarded in 1953 when Oxford University Press published the book and he was appointed dean of a new liberal arts college the University of California had established in Riverside.

Nisbet was excited by the idea of building a college from the ground up. The college opened its doors in 1954 with a faculty of 50 and a student body of 100. Nisbet reported that "we created a curriculum strong in the humanities, oriented toward small classes and the closest possible relationship between teacher and student, and as free as possible of the bureaucratized, large-scale, and increasingly regimented character that...was overtaking the American university with such speed after the Second World War" (MMS, 13). He spent the next ten years in full-time administration, interrupted by one "splendid, invigorating" year 1956-1957 when he went to Italy to take up residence as a visiting professor at the University of Bologna. There he rediscovered the joys of teaching, and partly for that reason, he left administration for good in 1963, when he took a one-year sabbatical at Princeton thanks to a Guggenheim Fellowship. He returned to Riverside to teach and to continue the writing he had begun at Princeton. Five books followed in quick succession: *The Sociological Tradition* (1966), *Tradition and Revolt* (1968), *Social Change and History* (1969), *The Social Bond* (1970), and *The Degradation of Academic Dogma: The University in America 1945-1970* (1971).

Nisbet left California in 1972 for the University of Arizona, where he joined both the history and sociology faculties. After forty years in the University of California system, he realized "that if I was not to run the risk of becoming an artifact, I had better get moving...." (MMS, 17). He published *The Social Philosophers* (1973) and *The Sociology of Emile Durkheim* (1974) while at Arizona, but he found the university much less intellectually stimulating than he had hoped. After two years in Tucson, Nisbet accepted the Albert Schweitzer Chair of the Humanities at Columbia, a position that allowed him again to teach in both the history and sociology departments. He had friends such as Robert Merton and Jacques Barzun at Columbia, and outside the university he enjoyed the friendship and neighborhood conviviality of Irving Kristol and Norman Podhoretz, among others. While at Columbia he published *Twilight of Authority*

(1975) and *Sociology as an Art Form* (1976). He enjoyed Columbia immensely but because he had vowed to leave the academy before growing old and unresponsive, he retired from teaching in 1978. Although he had been at Columbia for just four years, the university made him emeritus.

He moved to Washington, D.C., in 1978 to assume the post of resident scholar at the American Enterprise Institute (AEI). After two years, he retreated to full-time writing in his study at home (although he retained adjunct scholar status at AEI until 1986). Over the next few years, he revised and updated *The Social Philosophers* (1982); and he published *History of the Idea of Progress* (1980), *Prejudices: A Philosophical Dictionary* (1982), *Conservatism: Dream and Reality* (1986), *The Making of Modern Society* (1986), *Roosevelt and Stalin: A Failed Courtship* (1988), and *The Present Age: Progress and Anarchy in Modern America* (1988). His final book, *Teachers and Scholars*, a memoir of his Berkeley years, was published in 1992.

Nisbet also edited *Emile Durkheim: Selected Essays* (1965) and *Social Change* (1972). He co-edited *Contemporary Social Problems* (1961) with Robert Merton, and *History of Sociological Analysis* (1978) with Thomas Bottomore. An active scholar, he received numerous honors and awards, including the Award of Merit from the Republic of Italy, the Ingersoll Award for Scholarly Letters, and the 1988 Jefferson Lectureship. He served as the president of the Pacific Sociological Association, was for many years the social science editor for Oxford University Press, and was a fellow of the American Sociological Association, the American Philosophical Society, and the American Academy of Arts and Sciences. Both within and outside the United States, Nisbet is recognized by his admirers and detractors alike as one of the most original and influential American social theorists of his generation.

In his autobiographical introduction to *The Making of Modern Society*, Nisbet says that he hoped he would die over his typewriter "and that those close to me will call a taxidermist instead of a funeral undertaker, and that my mummified body will be suitably dressed and placed in proper position before the typewriter, available for display like the mummied remains of Jeremy Bentham in his room at the University of London." He continues, "Perhaps Berkeley, in some room on the fourth floor of Wheeler Hall, would be willing to provide permanent quarters. To my certain knowledge there are faculty members there at the present time who would prefer me back in that condition in my native grounds than alive and writing" (MMS, 22).

Professor Nisbet died September 9, 1996, three weeks short of his eighty-third birthday. Surviving him were his beloved wife Caroline, their daughter Ann, and two daughters from a previous marriage, Martha and Constance. His body did not make its way back to Wheeler Hall, but the corpus of his work is very much alive, a wonderful source of illumination for many, and, perhaps, a continuing source of irritation to the present occupants of Wheeler and other such halls.

CHAPTER TWO

COMMUNITY AND STATE POWER

A SINGLE SENTENCE in the preface to *The Quest for Community* summarizes both the aim of the book and what proved to be the master theme of Robert Nisbet's lifework. Nisbet says, "I have chosen to deal with the *political* causes of the manifold alienations that lie behind the contemporary quest for community" (QC, vii). He acknowledges that the "manifold alienations" that spur the desire for fellowship in community—the individual's sense of estrangement, isolation, or insecurity—stem from a variety of economic, religious, and moral changes. Still, he maintains, "the greatest single influence upon social organization in the modern West has been the developing concentration and power of the sovereign political State." He says that to "regard the State as simply a legal relationship, as a mere superstructure of power, is powerfully delusive." Instead, "The real significance of the modern State is inseparable from its successive penetrations of man's economic, religious, kinship and local allegiances, and its revolutionary dislocations of established centers of function and authority" (QC, viii). Individual "alienation" and preoccupation with community are manifestations of the decline of genuine communities created by the Western state.

The quest for community can take a variety of forms. It may lead to "easy religion," the psychiatrist's office, the cult, or the functionless ritualization of the past (QC, 31). But most commonly this quest today ends up in the political party or action group. "It is the image of community contained in the promise of the absolute, communal State that seems to have the greatest evocative power" (QC, 33). The dark irony, as Nisbet sees it, is that the search for community, itself caused by the state, often combines with the existing political power. Individuals seek "national community" whose vehicle is, of course, the state. Therefore, as communities wane, the desire for communal fellowship leads straight to the extension of state power—further eroding the communities that mediate between the individual and the state. It is a melancholy fate.

In Nisbet's view, "individualism" and the concentration of state power are not at odds; the slogan "Man versus the State," first used by Herbert Spencer, is faulty.[1] Nisbet argues, following Emile Durkheim, that the isolated, rights-bearing individual and the state are not in opposition because the individual needs the state to secure his rights (SED, 14-15, 148-150). The individual and the state are, however, each opposed to a third factor, namely "society." Nisbet notes that "social" was coined in the early nineteenth century when an old term was given new meaning. "Social, as a word, meant family, village, parish, town, voluntary association, and class, not the political state" (P, 287). "Society," as Nisbet uses the word, was composed of the welter of associations and communities that mediate individual experiences, that help fashion true "individuality" by providing stability, and that serve as hedges against the state. Of the two, society and the state, society is both prior to the state and much more important. As Alexis de Tocqueville observed, men create the state, but the communities that form society spring from the hand of God. These communities are not the product of conscious deliberation, planning, or individual reason. Indeed, manipulation by those who fail to comprehend their evolving, organic nature, can weaken and maim genuine communities. Society is never static and its pedigree is ancient. "Society," Nisbet says, paraphrasing Edmund Burke, "is a partnership of the dead, the living and the unborn" (TR, 23).

The contemporary crisis of community took more than four centuries to evolve. The medieval social world was rich in concrete communities in large measure because central state power was weak or nonexistent. Human needs and desires had to be fulfilled through cooperative effort. "The history of the Middle

Ages is one of the creation of groups to meet the needs left precarious by the fall of Rome. Patriarchal family, kindred, village community, walled town, guild, monastery, these are the relationships which had become strong in man's life by the time medieval Europe was at its zenith" (P, 51-52). If anything, there was a surfeit of *communitatum* in the Middle Ages. For much of the past four centuries the most evocative watchwords among the educated ("individual," "change," "interest," "progress," "freedom") described a condition quite different from our own—the wish to emancipate the individual from the inherited authority and status of traditional communities. Nonetheless, much of the West's modern social history has consisted in state power displacing traditional communities, which has resulted in the crisis of community and social alienation.

The following pages elaborate upon this theme. Discussed in turn are Nisbet's conceptions of community, political power, and the alienated or "loose" individual.

Community

The central modern problem, for Nisbet, is that of community—"community lost and community to be gained" (QC, vii). Certainly no term is of greater importance in Nisbet's work than "community." He uses it concretely, "in the hard sense the word enjoys in contemporary sociology" (DAD, 41). Although he makes regular references to medieval communities, there is nothing nostalgic, mystical, or romantic in his use of the term. The term refers neither to a "love compact"—although love (or hatred) may exist in community—nor to a direct, unmediated sense of "togetherness" or "belongingness." On the contrary, Nisbet asserts that no genuine, durable, and influential community has ever arisen on such feelings (DAD, 43). Community, to Nisbet, not only includes nonvisible spiritual or intellectual features, but also "the visible bonds, roles, statuses and norms of hierarchy and authority that provide boundary and also reinforcement to what is spiritually or intellectually contained within the community" (DAD, 41). For Nisbet, communities are real, substantial, and readily identifiable. Although some ascribe to "community" cosmic or almost talismanic qualities, Nisbet sees it as tangible and observable. Communities are human groups that spring up to fill perennial human needs and solve problems. To suppose that communities can exist solely through a telescopic humanitarian sentiment, or that they can vitalize themselves through indwelling affectual ties, without a concrete need or purpose, "is like supposing that the comradely ties of mutual aid which grow up incidentally in a military unit will long outlast a condition in which war is plainly and irrevocably banished" (QC, 61). As Nisbet says, quoting Ortega y Gasset, "Human beings do not come together to *be* together; they come together to *do something* together" (DAD, 43).

Specifically, Nisbet identifies several essential attributes of community. First, every community is built around some *func-tion*. The number of purposes or functions that have provided the bases of communities is without end. Functions may be noble or base, frivolous or profound, and range from crime to worship, from scholarship to child rearing. Communities are especially effective, though, when they are unfettered and au-tonomous in their efforts to achieve their own distinctive ends. Perfect autonomy is probably neither possible nor desirable, but the functions of communities are best realized without in-trusion from external sources (TA, 236). This is not to say that the functions of communities are immutable. Functions may change over time and are often sources of conflict *within* and *between* communities (QC, 88). Still, while particular communal functions may change, some function is essential to commu-nity. "Nothing is so likely in the long run to lead to the decay of community than the disappearance of the function that estab-lished it in the first place, or the failure of some commanding function to take the place of the first" (DAD, 43).

Second, a "community is strong in the sense of some tran-scending purpose, some ideal or ideals, or...some *dogma*" (DAD, 43). It is not enough for a community to have some function to perform. The function must be transformed into some deeply held belief. The function must "seem good"—the literal mean-ing of dogma (P, 92). Dogmas too may be good or evil but they are always profoundly held. Only then can they provide stability to a community and to the individuals within it. The individual cannot demonstrate all effectual and important truths; faith is required for action. The merely rational, calculating person will never be roused to action in a community. The decision to marry and rear children is not, for example, a rational calculus. Hence, the need for dogmas. As Cardinal Newman observed, "Men will die for a dogma who will not even stir for a conclusion" (quoted in ST, 233).

Third, community is characterized by *authority*, not power. "Communal authority, whether in family, monastery or university" rests "on some manifestation of consensus. Legitimacy, stated or otherwise, is of the essence" (DAD, 43-44). Typically, this authority comes about through habit, custom, use, and wont, not through some sort of conscious and explicit agreement. Indeed, Nisbet says, the nature of communal authority is such that merely "to follow the specifications of one's role" is "to engage in and be part of a pattern of authority" (SB, 142). Power, by contrast, is external and based upon force. It entails an effort to exact obedience or compliance of others to the will of one or more persons in a way *not* derived from the roles or statuses of the aggregate. Thus, power tends to be monistic and indiscriminate, with uniform effects, whereas authority by its nature is pluralistic, with multiform effects. Power arises, Nisbet says, only when authority breaks down.

Fourth, a community is *hierarchical*. By their nature, communities allow persons to know one another on a personal basis; yet within community, one's identity is inseparable from ones's role and status as governed by the norms of the whole community. "One is a member of a community as father, mother, priest, soldier, student or professor," and it is impossible to array such roles on a line of equality (DAD, 44). "There is no form of community that is without some form of stratification of function and role. Wherever two or more people associate, there is bound to be some form of hierarchy, no matter how variable, changing from one actor to the other, or how minor. Hierarchy is unavoidable to some degree" (TA, 238).

Fifth, community exhibits *solidarity*. "In a community it is almost instinctual for members to say 'we.' And one may trace the phases of dissolution of a community in the rising numbers of instances in which one is more likely to say 'I' than 'we'" (DAD, 44). One's identity in community is largely corporate, and the community as a whole has a "normative superiority" over each of its members. Such identity is possible to the degree to which a person feels a sense of duty to his role and to the community itself.

Sixth, any genuine community has a strong sense of *honor*. This sense is distinguished from utilitarian or pecuniary interests, and communities try to subordinate such interests to honor. "In the community of blood, kinship cannot be assessed in terms of either material or pecuniary interests.... And in the traditional community of scholars, in the university, one prided himself on an aloofness to the kinds of material or dollar interests that actuated businessmen"(DAD, 45). In community, "cash" and the "cash nexus" are terms of disapprobation. To pursue material interests alone is to bring dishonor to oneself in a community.

Finally, a community typically seeks to distance itself from the surrounding world and displays a sense of *superiority*. Communities are *in* the world, but they see themselves as not being *of* the world. According to Nisbet, this sense is perhaps as strongly felt among lowly communities as among the grand. "It is to be found within communities of the delinquent, the conspiratorial, even of the generations-old impoverished, as well as among guildsmen, knights and monks" (DAD, 56). Whatever its objective warrant, whether seen by others as pride or arrogance, a sense of collective superiority animates communities.

For much of history, communities—not individuals—were the irreducible units of society. In the Middle Ages, for example, honors, privileges, immunities, and freedoms attached to communities, not to individuals. One's identity and status depended upon one's communal membership: "Whether we are dealing with the family, the village, or the guild, we are in the presence of systems of authority and allegiance which were widely held to precede the individual in both origin and right." For example, "As many an institutional historian has discovered, medieval economy and law are simply unintelligible if we try to proceed from modern conceptions of individualism and contract. The group was primary" (QC, 81). The patriarchal and corporate family "was a fixed institutional system within which innumerable, indispensable functions were performed." Taxes were levied and honors bestowed on the family, not the individual. "In its corporate solidarity lay the ground for almost all decisions affecting the individual—his occupation, welfare, marriage and the rearing of his children." Similarly, agriculture was essentially communal, and the medieval town "was itself a close association, and its members—*citizens* in the medieval sense— were bound to live up to its articles and customs almost as rigorously as the peasants on the manor." Towns were, in fact, associations of associations. Innumerable communities lay within them—guilds and small associations for mutual aid, religious faith, and political responsibility (QC, 81-83).

Measured institutionally, large sectors of Western society remained "medieval" well into the nineteenth century, and, of course, traditional social unities persist even today. But, as early as the sixteenth century, many medieval communities began to decline. We were then at "the beginning of a world in which the individual—the artist, scientist, the man of business, the politician and the religious devotee—becomes steadily more detached, in area after area, from the close confinements of kinship, church and association" (QC, 86). Echoes of modern views of community could be heard as early as the sixteenth century, and to the modern mind, the essential attributes of community were often perceived in negative terms. To this mind, communities were often *particularistic, parochial, exclusive, authoritarian, arrogant, intolerant,* and *inegalitarian.* The measure of the decline of communities is the same as that of the emancipation of the individual; and the disruption of community is commensurate with the rise of the individual—his secularism, mobility, and moral freedom. "We can not, in sum, deal with the progressive emancipation of individuals without recognizing also the decline of those structures from which the individual has been emancipated" (QC, 76). The social history of this transition contains a variety of economic, moral, and religious changes. Yet standing behind each of these is a revolutionary system of power and rights; according to Nisbet, "This system is the political State" (QC, 97).

Political Power: From the War State to the Welfare State

Nisbet reflects Max Weber in defining the state "in terms of the specific means peculiar to it, as to every political association, namely the use of physical force" (SB, 384). The state did not emerge, says Nisbet, as a direct outgrowth of family, tribe, and local community as had been supposed by social evolutionists since Aristotle proposed his triadic evolutionary scheme of family to village to *polis,* or state (TA, 153). Whether in ancient Athens and Rome, or in modern England and France, the historical evidence suggests that the "rise and aggrandizement of political States took place in circumstances of powerful opposition to kinship and other traditional authorities" (QC, 100). Foremost among these circumstances was the condition of war.

War, the seed of the political state, was not, Nisbet believes, the "war of every man against every man" envisioned by Thomas Hobbes in the natural, asocial condition, for no such condition ever existed. Nisbet agrees with David Hume's characterization of the asocial "natural condition" as a "philosophical fiction."[2] Indeed, Nisbet echoes Hume's famous account of the origins of government in band warfare. Hume observed, "Government commences more casually and more imperfectly" than is typically supposed. "It is probable that the first ascendant of one man over multitudes began during a state of war...and if the chieftain possessed as much equity as prudence and valor, he became, during peace, the arbiter of all differences, and could gradually by a mixture of force and consent, establish his authority."[3] As Nisbet puts it, "Everywhere the state, as we first encounter it in history, is simply the institutionalization, and projection to wider areas of function and authority, of the command-tie that in the beginning binds only the warrior-leader and his men" (1986, xxi). Hume's "force," according to Nisbet, is focused initially upon the authority and function of family and kindred. The warring state and the family wax and wane inversely. Thus, for example, Nisbet records that "Homer offers us the picture in his *Iliad* and *Odyssey* of a Greek society just beginning to face the pangs of conflict between its age-old kinship structure and the pressing needs of war. Eventually the political state won out. In Athens this victory was dramatized by the famous Cleisthenean Reforms, which abolished the ancient kinship structure and brought in the city-state built from the start on sovereignty, individualism and preponderance of contractual ties" (1986, xxi-xxii).

Similarly, Nisbet says, Roman history "is one long saga of conflict between established *patria potestas*, the sacred and imprescriptible sovereignty of the family in its own affairs, and the *imperium militiae*, the power vested in military leaders over their troops" (1986, xxii). When the empire replaced the republic, the *imperium* triumphed over traditional kinship society, and during the next several centuries the Roman state consolidated its victory. When Augustus became Pontifex Maximus, he unified Roman civil and religious life and substituted Caesar worship for the traditional household lares and penates; parental privilege over the marriages of their children shrank to a conditional veto; and the capacity of the *paterfamilias* to administer and sell property was greatly curtailed. "By the fifth century, the once-proud Roman family had been ground down by the twin forces of centralization and atomization…" (1986, xxiii).

In the sixth century the Institutes of Justinian codified the legal changes that had occurred over the centuries, and, as Nisbet reminds us, "Roman law as we know it in the Institutes of Justinian is preeminently the law of the strong military state" (TA, 166). Fundamental to this law were the ideas of *sovereignty, concession,* and *contract.* Under the Roman code, the sovereign is deemed above the law and the sole source of the law; no group or association can claim legal existence without the approval of the sovereign; and "no relationship among individuals, however ancient, however sacred in tradition, however useful, can claim the sanction of the state unless it is shown to have emanated from the willing assent of free actors" (TA, 170-171).

The rediscovery of the Justinian Code during the revival of learning in the late Middle Ages and the Renaissance helped shape civil law throughout Europe. Nisbet remarks, "It is no exaggeration to say that Western society has been twice Romanized" (TA, 166). Moreover, in "striking degree the effects of war and of the military on modern society have been registered through a political and legal system constructed out of Romanist elements" (TA, 167). In any event, in modern, as in pre-modern, societies, war has helped the state aggrandize power. Put otherwise, the state is essentially the institutionalization of the power of war, or, as Randolph Bourne put it, war is "the health of the state" (TA, 154). Accordingly, as Tocqueville observed, men of military genius are fond of centralization and centralizers are fond of war.[4] War is the prime force in concentrating authority within the central organ of the state. This concentration is achieved largely through individualizing social aggregates. "Only through the State's penetration of traditional social authorities to the individuals who live under them can its authority be said to be manifest" (SB, 385). Traditional authorities tend to be multiple, concentric, and autonomous. Under the mandates of war, they must be subordinated, even humiliated. "[T]o the military function is added, in time, other functions of a legal, judicial, economic, and even religious nature, and, over a long period, we can see the passage of the State from an exclusively military association to one incorporating almost every aspect of human life" (QC, 101).

In times of war, moreover, individuals often abandon their "smaller patriotisms" for *amor patriae*, love of the fatherland. War provides the most intense sense of community, "the kind of community that is brought into existence by emergency and then reinforced by shared values and emotions which reach the depths of human nature" (P, 309). War also disturbs "the cake of custom, the net of tradition" because it favors innovation, science, and technological invention (PA, 6; P, 309-311). But the most portentous effect of war is perhaps its democratizing tendency. "Democracy, in all its variants, is the child of war" (P, 312). For example: the Cleisthenean Reforms mentioned above ushered in the first-known democracy; the social character of Imperial Rome—"its greater moral and intellectual freedom, its closer and closer relation between the emperor and the masses, and its large number of entitlements to citizens"—resulted from what began as privileges for war veterans; and, as observed by persons as different as the Marquis de Condorcet and H. A. Taine, the mass infantry that came about in the Middle Ages led directly to modern democracy and egalitarianism. The step from conscript to democratic "citizen" is small and virtually inevitable. Nisbet observes, "Most of the great wars in the modern West have been attended by gains in the political and social rights of citizenship as well as by increased nationalism and centralization of power" (MMS, 133).

Democratization also has affected the nature of war. According to Nisbet, the intensity and range of war have increased in the twentieth century because war has become more and more identified with popular, moral aspirations: freedom, democracy, self-determination, and justice. "When the goals and values of a war are *popular* both in the sense of mass participation and spiritual devotion, the historic, institutional *limits* of war tend to recede further and further into the void." War has become spiritualized and infused with great moral purpose by modern nation-states. "It is now something more nearly akin to the Crusades of medieval Europe, but in the name of nation rather than the Church" (QC, 39). Such lofty purpose, Nisbet maintains, has allowed the regimentation and bureaucratization that have always been part of organized warfare to penetrate wider and wider social and cultural areas of life. The tragedy of contemporary war, according to Nisbet, is not that its efficiency has become progressively destructive, but rather "that the stifling regimentation and bureaucratic centralization of military organization is becoming more and more the model of associative and leadership relationships in time of peace and in nonmilitary organizations" (QC, 43).

Tocqueville noted the affinity among war, democratic egalitarianism, and the centralization of state power, and saw that egalitarianism and the centralization of power were the two dominant tendencies of modern Western history. Like Tocqueville, Nisbet fully appreciated equality before the law and equality of opportunity. But also like Tocqueville he saw the danger of equality of condition or equality of result, for this type of equality seeks uniformity and homogeneity through the power of the state. The irony of this type of equality for both Tocqueville and Nisbet was that the passion for equality and an awareness of inequality were enhanced, not diminished, by more equal conditions. As Nisbet observed, "Equality feeds on itself as no other single social value does. It is not long before it becomes more than a value. It takes on…all the overtones of redemptiveness and becomes a religious rather than a secular idea" (TA, 202). And, of course, "All that has magnified equality of condition has necessarily tended to abolish or diminish the buffers to central power which are constituted by social classes, kindreds, guilds and other groups whose virtual essence is hierarchy" (TA, 209).

The passion for equality leads to the centralization of power, and, in turn, this centralization fosters the spirit of equality. In this regard, Tocqueville again served as Nisbet's guide. Tocqueville argued in *The Old Regime and the French Revolution* that administrative centralization was an institution of the old regime and that the revolution and Napoleon merely perfected what the monarchy had begun. Under the French monarchy in the seventeenth and eighteenth centuries, the ancient intermediate powers, both political and civil, were supplanted one after another by the state, creating a condition "in which men were as much alike and their statuses as equal as possible."[5] In Nisbet's words, "the very centralization of monarchical and State power could not help but create the conditions for a growing interest in personal equality. For, in the interests of its own aggrandizement, the State was forced to restrict sharply the authority of medieval classes and estates. In so doing it could not help but partially level these ranks and, by its growing stress upon the impersonality and equality of law, to create a scene in which many traditional medieval inequalities had to be diminished" (QC, 107-108).

The centralization of state power of which Nisbet speaks is significant for another reason. As already noted, Nisbet sees that economic and other changes have contributed to the decline of community. Yet behind these changes, Nisbet says, was the centralization of state power. Capitalism, for example, disturbed many traditional social unities, but, Nisbet argues, the rise of nation-states preceded and made possible the existence of capitalism. He asserts, "The State's development of a single system of law, sanctioned by military power, to replace the innumerable competing laws of guild, Church and feudal principality; its deliberate cultivation of trade in the hinterland; its standardized systems of coinage, weights and measures; its positive subsidies and protections to those new businessmen who were seeking to operate outside the framework of guild and Church; its creation of disciplined State workhouses—all provided a powerful political stimulus to the rise of capitalism" (QC, 105). Capitalism is impossible to imagine outside the context of the nation-state, itself the product of innumerable changes in the structure of political power.

As important as the state was to the emergence of capitalism, ironically, the continual distension of state power undermines and threatens capitalism. In its early stages, Nisbet suggests, the development of capitalism—freedom of contract, fluidity of capital, mobility of labor, and the factory system—relied upon the stability provided by "the continued existence of institutional and cultural allegiances which were, in every sense, precapitalist." Capitalism, to maintain its health, needed what traditional associations and communities could provide—moral capital, motivations, and cultural order. As Nisbet puts it, "Most of the relative stability of nineteenth-century capitalism arose from the fact of the very *incompleteness* of the capitalist revolution" (QC, 237). This was Joseph Schumpeter's point when he argued that "the family and the family home used to be the mainspring of the typical bourgeois kind of profit motive." The genuine bourgeois entrepreneur and capitalist did not work and save "from the rational self-interest of the detached individual" but rather for the future well-being of "his wife and children."[6] But, over time, family motives became rare, and individuals more detached. And this, according to Nisbet, was due largely to the extension of state power, for "The alleged disorganization of the modern family is, in fact, simply an erosion of its natural authority, the consequence, in considerable part, of the absorption of its functions by other bodies, chiefly the state" (1962, xii-xiii).

Nisbet agrees with many others that the waning of the bourgeois profit motive and the loss of family functions stem in large measure from the rise of the welfare state. But what Nisbet stresses is quite novel—the integral connection between the war state and the welfare state and the role of intellectuals in making this connection. War, he suggests, nourishes the historic goals of secular humanitarianism. "[I]t is in time of war that many of the reforms, first advocated by socialists, have been accepted by capitalist governments and made parts of the structures of their societies. Equalization of wealth, progressive taxation, nationalization of industries, the raising of wages and improvements in working conditions, worker-management councils, housing ventures, death taxes, unemployment insurance plans, pension systems, and the enfranchisement of formerly voteless elements of the population have all been, in one country or another, achieved or advanced under the impress of war" (QC, 40). In *Twilight of Authority* Nisbet estimates that in the last two centuries 75 percent of all national programs in Western countries designed to equalize income, property, and opportunity "have been in the first instance adjuncts of the war state and of the war economy" (TA, 220).

Concerning America, Nisbet argues that, although the full flowering of the welfare state occurred in the last three or four decades, its roots were in World War I and Woodrow Wilson. According to Nisbet, Wilson's "political, economic, social and intellectual reorganization of America in the short period 1917-1919 is one of the most extraordinary feats in the long history of war and polity…. Within a few short months he had transformed traditional, decentralized, regional and localist America into a war state that at its height permeated every aspect of life" (PA, 42-43). Congress agreed to Wilson's request for war powers, in Nisbet's words, "beyond the dream of a Caesar." Wages, prices, and profits were controlled by the national government; mines and railroads were nationalized along with the telephone and telegraph industries; and civil liberties were suspended. Nisbet asserts flatly: "I believe it no exaggeration to say that the West's first real experience with totalitarianism—political absolutism extended into every possible area of culture and society, education, religion, industry, the arts, local community and family included, with a kind of terror always waiting in the wings—came with the American war state under Woodrow Wilson" (TA, 183).

Wilson's programs were the offsprings of progressive intellectuals such as Herbert Croly, Walter Lippmann, and John Dewey who saw the social possibilities of war. And, although the idea of a national community slumbered during the 1920s, the idea was easily resuscitated during the New Deal. Nisbet says, "to a large degree, the so-called New Deal was no more than an assemblage of governmental structures modeled on those which had existed in 1917.... And it has to be admitted that in the United States it was those aspects of the New Deal—NRA, AAA, WPA, and the CCC among them—with the most overtones of war-inspired militance, of centralization and collectivism, that clearly had the greatest attraction for our intellectual class" (TA, 184-185; see also RS, 91-110, on the Wilson/Roosevelt connection).

The New Deal did not do much for unemployment, but it did provide the "moral equivalent of war" and advanced the idea of national community. It was World War II that ended the Depression, but, of course, it also gave tremendous impetus to the idea of a national community, not only as a good community, but as the only possible community. As Nisbet says, the "novel effect of World War II was the creation of formal, official—and lasting!—union between the intellectual and the national government, at least when the latter could be thought of as in trustworthy hands, like Wilson's or FDR's" (TA, 185). The Cold War followed, and the tie between intellectuals and the national government became even firmer. "Political omnicompetence, with the state the spearhead of all social and cultural life; industrialization, however farcical in context; nationalization of education; rampant secularism; and growing consumer-hedonism—all this bespeaks modernity to the Western clerisy and the welcome sign of the developed, the progressive" (PA, 73).

The idea of a national community reached its zenith in the 1960s and early 1970s. During the Kennedy and Johnson administrations, "the best and the brightest" planned the Vietnam War (only to see the political clerisy turn against "the intellectual's war"). Motivated in part by a desire to deflect criticism from the action in Vietnam, Johnson announced his "War on Poverty," a phrase he chose because "war" conjured images of national purpose and unity. The "Great Society" programs that fueled this effort embodied the progressive dream of a nation mobilized to seek Jeffersonian communal ends through Hamiltonian strong-state means.

Nisbet notes that the political community has been held

somewhat at bay since the mid-1970s (TA, 3-74). However, once a bureaucracy is created it "neither dies nor fades away" (P, 32). Still, whatever the future of the idea of a national community might be, the twentieth-century transformation of intellectuals has been remarkable. In the nineteenth century, Nisbet notes, Socialist and liberal intellectuals were as wary of the state as conservatives: socialists, including Marx, targeted the state as the first object of revolutionary wrath and believed the state would "wither away" under socialism; and, for their part, liberals were opposed to the state because it represented the chief threat to freedom (PA, 61-62). Today these ideologies are mainstays of the centralized, bureaucratic national state. This transformation, Nisbet argues persuasively, began with war and has been sustained by subsequent wars and by the many equivalents of war.

The Loose Individual

The tightening of power at the center, Nisbet says, unbinds the threads of the social fabric. Society is left with many "loose individuals," loose "in the sense of the loose cannon, the ship that slips its hawser, the dog its leash, the individual his accustomed moral restraints." A rising number of Americans today are "loose from marriage and the family, from the school, the church, the nation, job and moral responsibility" (PA, 84). Lacking institutional and associative resources these individuals are thrown back upon their inner resources, prey to amorphous feelings of anxiety and guilt. In *The Present Age*, Nisbet says, such persons are prone to "alienation," "subjectivism" and "permissiveness." To mediate their relations with others they bank on the "cash nexus" and hedonistic calculations. Yet they are devoid of the social assets required for genuine individuality and creativity.

By "alienation" Nisbet does not mean disaffection from the social order—one need not be alienated to repudiate society. The term, as Nisbet uses it, refers to two distinct but closely related phenomena: first, one's relationship to oneself and, second, one's relationship to the impersonal institutions of modern society. Regarding the first, "uprooted, alone, without secure status, cut off from community or any system of clear moral purpose," the individual is "metaphysically beleaguered, as it were." In the place of community, there are "vast institutions and organizations" that fragment the individual "into the mechanical roles he is forced to play, none of them touching his innermost self but all of them separating man from this self, leaving him, so to speak, existentially missing in action." In the second and related sense of alienation, the emphasis is upon society which, because of its impersonal and bureaucratic institutions, seems to the individual remote, incomprehensible, or fraudulent (ST, 265-266). In this sense, "Alienated behavior is a form of withdrawal of energy from social ends and purposes. It occurs when individuals believe themselves powerless to influence their own lives or the lives of others or when the ends of a social order, or its forms of relationship, seem hopelessly remote, alien or meaningless" (SB, 264-265).

Alienation to some degree can occur within every sphere of activity; no social type or occupation is completely immune. But Nisbet says, "it is probably true that more alienation tends to exist within the broad category we call 'intellectuals' than, for example, within the categories of automobile mechanics, carpenters or even lawyers and physicians" (SB, 266). The same can also be said of "subjectivism"—those who incline toward it are more "educated." What Nisbet calls "subjectivism" tends to be self-doting, a "wholehearted concern with feelings, emotion, awareness, and awareness of awareness of self, the me, the ego." It is opposed to a rational orientation to a discernible and objective external world. Yet, Nisbet goes on, the word "subjectivism" gives only a whiff of "the modern age of self-spelunking, ego-diving and awareness intoxication" (P, 243), as indicated by the pervasiveness of psychobabble—the language of subjectivism. As pervasive as it is, subjectivism is especially common among academics. Campus novelists and playwrights write of nothing but themselves and make "small fortunes out of public exposure of their psychogenitalia" (P, 243). Literary theorists employ "deconstruction" which, despite a pretentious glaze on its psychobabble, is merely a "technique of reducing the great to the merely subjective, the solipsistic" (PA, 130). And the number of social scientists for whom "objectivity is either a delusion or something inherently repugnant" rises constantly. "There is widespread retreat to all the diverse forms of subjectivism which hold up preoccupation with and study of one's self as the beginning of true wisdom" (HIP, 347). Typical is Alvin Gouldner, one of the mandarins of sociology, who claimed that the ultimate goal of sociology is "the deepening of the sociologist's own awareness of who and what he is in a specific society at a given time" (quoted in PA, 128).

The social sciences, along with Freudian psychology and progressive education, have also contributed to the malady Nisbet calls "permissiveness" by promoting a loose morality epitomized in the epigram "To understand all is to pardon all." These fields have removed responsibility from individuals and shifted it either to uncontrollable impulses or to society as a whole. This, of course, promotes "permissiveness," the moral equivalent of subjectivism's epistemological relativism. Yet these fields are not the original cause of this malady. The state, through dislocation and preemption, is the primary cause of permissiveness, according to Nisbet. The natural authority of the family, school, local court, and local community has been eroded by the insatiable bureaucratic state. We are left with parents who cower before their children, teachers who ingratiate themselves with students, and judges who refuse to impose proper judgment. "Such permissiveness is not the cause, but the result, of the breakdown of authority" (P, 236). Ultimately, though, the dislocation of natural authority by state power is attributable to equality. "True liberty...turns into license or permissiveness when liberty is obliged to fuse with equality" (P, 238). In an age jealous of all rank, in which envy is boundless, to be authoritative, to exert discipline, is to risk recriminations and reprisals.

When function and authority were gathered into society's central organ, it degraded traditional dogmas, says Nisbet. "Values such as love, honor and loyalty do not, cannot thrive, in a sociological vacuum" (TR, 130). They must be cultivated in groups small enough to instill learning and meaningful enough to the individual to convey to him the profound significance to those values. Without such groups, without higher and ennobling purposes, Nisbet says, money becomes the common denominator in human relations, the "marketplace" becomes the setting for more and more relationships, and people develop a narcotic-like fascination with money. Cash payment, as Thomas Carlyle wrote, becomes "the sole nexus between man and man." Nisbet takes it from there: "Every act of service, responsibility, protection and aid to others is an act presupposing or calling for monetary exchange, for cash payment" (PA, 86). The cash nexus—which can be seen in sports, the arts, entertainment, and organized religion—has transformed the traditional locations of profit and property. For example, "real" or "several" property such as land, buildings, machines—the objects pursued by traditional entrepreneurs in order to endow a family legacy—has given way progressively to "soft property" such as cash, and stocks—the lifeblood of casino capitalism and the modern wheel of fortune. In such pursuits, "morality becomes expendable" (PA, 84-95).

Nisbet's most elaborate example of the abasement of dogma and the rise of the cash nexus, however, is his analysis of the university in *The Degradation of Academic Dogma*. By virtue of its structure and dogma, the university was until World War II the most medieval institution in the modern world. Its college structure, its hierarchy, and its roles of professor, scholar, dean, provost, and chancellor had changed little over almost eight centuries. Similarly, its dogma—the pursuit of knowledge for its own sake—had animated and preserved scholarship and teaching in the university since the dogma was fashioned in the twelfth and thirteenth centuries at Bologna, Paris, and Oxford. But, according to Nisbet, all of this began to change in America immediately after World War II when very large "direct grants from government and foundation to individual members of university faculties or small company-like groups of faculty members" led to semi-autonomous campus research institutes, centers, and bureaus. This money created what Nisbet calls a new breed of "academic bourgeoisie" and "new men of power" who withdrew from the traditional university departmental structure and eschewed scholarship and teaching to pursue big-money research. They became the envy of others, and by the 1960s the cash motive ruled supreme among university faculties. Increasingly, faculty members were hired (not appointed) according to their grant-getting capacity, not their capacity for scholarship and teaching, and they were subsequently evaluated according to the same criterion. Interest replaced honor. The student, meanwhile, was served with "a new dedication to his needs, his identity, his ego, his peace of mind." New "cults" replaced the old university community, cults that ranged "from silent communion in the forms of sensitivity, encounter, and 'feel' courses run by students all the way to entire new colleges within universities, even whole campuses, dedicated to helping the student solve what is fashionably known as 'identity crises'" (DAD, 113). The cash nexus and "the triumph of the therapeutic" have the same origin and complement one another.[7]

The lives of "loose individuals" are easily justified in doctrines dating from the seventeenth and eighteenth centuries. According to them, creativity and progress require that the rational individual should be released from restrictive social relationships. These doctrines will be treated more fully in the next chapter. But let me note here that Nisbet agrees that the freedom of persons is crucial to creative and intellectual achievement. All great works are the concrete result of personal performance (QC, 233). But it is not equally true that intellectual and cultural achievements are the sole result of individual effort and social separation. It is, rather, the individual genius's relationship to "his locality, his religion or the various other communal influences that give his work inspiration and direction" (QC, 234). Neither freedom nor achievement can be separated from community—from the contexts of authentic individuality. The "crucial sparks igniting the blaze of creativity that goes into the golden ages" of history, Nisbet says, arise from cultures with sacred cores against which secular forces are pitted; they are strong in the sense of community against which an emergent and dynamic individualism clashes; and they are animated by the struggle between hierarchy and equality.

These, of course, are not the conditions we know. The present age in America is long on secularism, individualism, and equality; but without the solid wall of religion, community, and hierarchy, there is nothing from which to be freed. "The stimulating conflict of ideas and values found in [golden] ages is gone from American culture..." (P, 149-151). Gone, too, are the very sources of individuality. What obtains is the isolated individual who yearns for community but for whom the charms of family, religion, and civic association often pale before the luster of the unified state.

CHAPTER THREE

POLITICAL MONISM AND SOCIAL PLURALISM

"IDEAS HAVE CONSEQUENCES."[1] So Richard Weaver believed and Robert Nisbet agreed. Indeed, Nisbet maintained that "everything vital in history reduces itself ultimately to ideas, which are the motive forces.... Above all, man is what he thinks the transcending moral values are in his life and in the lives of those around him" (TA, 233). Changes in the nature of political sovereignty cannot occur, therefore, without changes in intellectual and moral beliefs. Consequently, in addition to the social history of community and political sovereignty surveyed in the preceding chapter, Nisbet's different works contain a history of the ideas that have both contributed to, and mirrored, the changes in community and sovereignty. This Nisbet does chiefly through portraits of two great traditions in Western social and political thought. In the first, presaged by Plato, the emphasis on the political virtually extinguishes all other associations. The dis-

tinction between state and society is either denied, or it is deemed
that society should be subordinated to the state because of its
tendencies to conflict and oppression. "Such groups as family,
locality, neighborhood, church, and other autonomous associations are almost uniformly reduced to their individual atoms,
made into unities dependent upon concession of existence by
the state, or in some other way significantly degraded" (TA, 245).
In the modern era, this is the tradition of Hobbes, Rousseau,
Bentham, Lenin, and "numberless members of the political clerisy
of our own day," the tradition of "political monism."

The second tradition, that of "social pluralism," begins with
Aristotle and includes Burke, Tocqueville, Acton, Lammenais,
Proudhon, and Kropotkin. It maintains a clear distinction between state and society and conceives true freedom as proceed-
ing "less from what the actual constitution of the political order
proper may prescribe than from the relationship that exists between the political state, whatever its form of government, and
the several institutions of the social sphere" (TA, 245-246). According to this tradition, no state is deemed free if the government rules over the social, economic, and intellectual spheres.
"Conversely, a government monarchical or oligarchical in structure can be a free government if—as has been the case many
times in history—it respects the other institutions of society
and permits autonomies accordingly in the social and economic
spheres" (TA, 246).

Nisbet's chief concern is with theories of sovereignty and social association that have arisen over the past four hundred years. In this chapter, I will partially reconstruct his portraits of these two traditions with special emphasis upon the monists, Hobbes and Rousseau, and the pluralists, Burke and Tocqueville. Nonetheless, because Plato and Aristotle anticipated much subsequent thinking, Nisbet began his analysis of these traditions with these two thinkers.

Plato and Aristotle

Plato, Nisbet notes, lived and wrote "during the waning years of what is generally regarded as the most golden of the golden ages in the history of culture; the fifth century B.C. in ancient Athens" (SP, 2). Early in the century the Greeks had defeated the Persians at the battle of Marathon, and Athens had established the first known democracy. In 404 B.C., however, Athens endured a humiliating defeat at the hands of the Spartans, who helped destroy the Athenian assembly and establish a small oligarchy that came to be known as the Dictatorship of Thirty. Although the licentiousness of democracy greatly troubled Plato, he said the new government "made the former government look like an age of gold." Plato concluded that existing forms of government were "beyond redemption" and that only "correct philosophy" could afford "a vantage point from which we can discern in all cases what is just for communities and individuals." This philosophy, especially as conveyed in *The Republic*, Nisbet says, "had the effect of making the ideal of politics, of political power, of the political bond, of the political community, the most distinctive and most influential of all types of community to be found in Western philosophy" (SP, 3).

Nisbet believed that the specific form of this political philosophy was shaped by three features of Plato's thought. First, his "social developmentalism," as presented in the third book of *The Laws;* second, his distinction between appearance (which involves the senses and ordinary experience) and reality (known to reason alone); and third, his distinction between nature and convention. For Plato, in "the chain of being, the political community ranks highest in this world among all communities; it is the result of a long process of development; it is man's associative *reality*, in contrast to the merely spurious and superficially attractive; and, finally, it is in its perfect condition the mode of community most natural to man" (SP, 4-5). Plato's ideal political community is therefore conceived to be not merely true by the lights of pure reason, but also good, beautiful, and just. Thus, Plato is the "true source" of what Nisbet calls "political mysticism." He sought "the kind of community that would be in harmony with the needs and aspirations of men, that would reflect a timeless truth and that would be attainable wherever there were men of rationality and goodness" (SP, 7-8).

More concretely, in *The Republic,* Plato proposed an ideal political community wherein "the guardians" would rule. This class comprised philosopher-kings and warriors—the best in reason and the best in "spiritedness" or *thymos.* The guardians would rule over all others—the economic class—because these others were deficient in reason and *thymos*; they were motivated by base passions and desires. The main features of this political community were conveyed, Nisbet said, through a description of the four demands Plato made of the guardians: *asceticism, absolute communism, a monolithic power structure,* and *militarism.* The guardians must be ascetic because the harmony and unity of Plato's ideal polity depended on the capacity of the rulers to submit their private and individual interests to the common good. Indeed, Plato believed that private interest and social factions were quite simply *the* evils the ideal political community was designed to overcome. Absolute communism was required in order to elevate the needs of the political community above those of the individuals. Plato prescribed "communal property, community dwelling places, communal pursuits—and especially—communal sex and child rearing" (SP, 14). The political structure of the guardians had to be monolithic because the forms of authority and function outside the polity could only lead to faction and divisive loyalties. And, finally, militarism was an essential feature of the guardians in Plato's ideal polity because courage, aggressiveness, and boldness in battle were needed both to defend the *polis* or city-state and to ensure internal cohesion.

According to Nisbet, the inspiration for Plato's vision was not nostalgia for a dim past of Athens, as Sir Karl Popper and others have suggested.[2] Had it been so, Plato "would surely have given us something approximating the kinship society that had, in fact, existed and that Plato so brilliantly described in his evolutionary account of primitive society in the third book of *The Laws.*" Instead, kinship is abolished among the guardians by Plato and "the social and juridical features of kinship society such as decentralization, concentric circles of membership, gerontocracy, tradition and the like are utterly absent" (SP, 9). Rather than nostalgia, Nisbet says, what animated Plato "is a blend of rigorous social nihilism and political affirmation" (SP, 8). All social extra-political sources of authority that might compete with the polity are swept away by Plato in order to ensure a unified political community.

This unity is opposed by Aristotle. As Nisbet observes, "It is difficult to imagine two minds more unlike than Plato and Aristotle. Aristotle is as down-to-earth and empirical as Plato is transcendental; as pluralist in his view of politics as Plato is monist." Plato's mind was that of a rationalist and a religious poet, whereas Aristotle was the patient observer, the scholar, and researcher. "We find Plato...rich in appeal to pure reason, in intuitive boldness and in revolutionary impulse...whereas we find Aristotle rich in the opposite of these qualities, appealing to observation, experience, tradition, and study rather than pure insight" (SP, 16). Whereas Plato is the first and arguably the greatest political philosopher, Aristotle is "the first real social scientist," according to Nisbet. In Aristotle's *Politics,* "we find some of the wisest, most astute, and learned observations on the nature of community to be found anywhere in Western history" (SP,18, 22).

In Book II of the *Politics,* Aristotle analyzes Plato's conception of the unity or oneness of the polity. Aristotle states that "the city is in its nature a sort of multitude." To seek too much unity is to transform the city into a family and a family into an individual. "So even if one were able to do this, one ought not do it, as it would destroy the city." The unity that obtains in the *polis* or city is not one of homogeneity but of heterogeneity, according to Aristotle. "[A] city does not arise from persons who are similar." More unity in the city is not achieved by making everyone a shoemaker or by making everyone a carpenter; the city or *polis* requires differentiation and a division of labor. "It is evident," Aristotle says, "from these things, then, that the city is not naturally one in this sense as some argue and what was said to be the greatest good for the cities actually destroys them."

Aristotle states that even if unity in the city were desirable, it does not follow that unity obtains when "all say 'mine' and 'not mine' at the same time." He is deeply apprehensive over Plato's community of property, wives, and children. Regarding property, he says, "What belongs in common to the most people is accorded the least care; they take thought for their own things above all, and less about things common or only so much as falls to them individually." Similarly, with regard to Plato's community of wives and children, Aristotle says that such relationships would be watery and diluted. Individuals would not be devoted to all but indifferent to each. "For there are two things above all which make human beings cherish and feel affection, what is one's own and what is dear; and neither of these can be available to those who govern themselves in this way."[3] Moreover, Aristotle notes, those who seek communal oneness eliminate the very basis of friendship—doing favors for friends or guests.

Given the empirical cast of Aristotle's mind, he cannot say that there is a single best regime. His research told him that rule by the one, by the few, or by the many may be virtuous or vicious. Nonetheless, this same cast of mind leads Aristotle to certain prudential judgments. In any political community, various people will lay claim to authority—the many, the rich, the virtuous, the one best—and each of their claims is likely to possess a measure of legitimacy. Consequently, Aristotle says, the polity that accommodates a plurality of claims will be the most just. Mixed and balanced regimes that recognize and maintain differences, not unity, are most salutary. Thus, a regime in which the richest of the poor and the poorest of the rich rule is superior to one where the rich rule or one where the poor rule.

In these differences between Plato and Aristotle, Nisbet says, "we have the essence of the difference which has survived throughout Western thought down to the present moment"—the difference between monism and pluralism (SP, 22).

Monism

Although there are many modern monistic theories of sovereignty and association, in various works Nisbet chooses Hobbes and Rousseau as archetypical. In fact, Nisbet calls them "the prime catalytic agents" in modern political thinking. Like Plato, Hobbes and Rousseau developed political philosophies that were "a blend of social nihilism and political affirmation." And "the affirmation in each instance is the state conceived as being, not force, not repression, but justice, freedom, and tranquility for the individual" (SP, 10).

It is tempting to say that the images of human nature and the political order found in Hobbes's *Leviathan,* published in 1651, are artifacts of his mode of inquiry. Hobbes claimed to be inspired by Galileo, who followed the "resolutive-compositive" method. All assertions Hobbes makes about human nature are designed to "resolve" or isolate the elementary passions or desires he believes set autonomous individuals in motion; his method of analysis commits him to an asocial view of human nature. From his resolutive analysis of the passions, described in the first twelve chapters of *Leviathan*, Hobbes deduces in chapter 13 what he calls the "natural condition," one devoid of the influences of "civilization." The rest of *Leviathan* uses the "compositive" method and analyzes the "commonwealth" or political society, the essential remedy to the extraordinary inconveniences of the natural condition. Hobbes's metaphysical or deductive method, therefore, wipes clean the influences of history and civilization in the "resolutive" phase of his method in order to compose or construct the ideal political order in his "compositive" phase.

What prompts action, what motivates human beings, Hobbes states, is their appetites and aversions. There is no *summum bonum*. Nothing, for Hobbes, is intrinsically good or evil. The objects of desire are "good"; the objects of aversion are "evil."[4] The capacity to attain our appetites or desires Hobbes calls "power," and he asserts that it is "a generall inclination of all mankind, a perpetuall and restlesse desire of Power after Power, that ceaseth only with Death."[5] Although our aversions are many, the chief evil we naturally fear is death itself. Our combined appetites and aversions lead us in the natural condition— the condition without a common superior to overawe us—to a state of perpetual war; "and such a warre, as is of every man against every man."[6] For, Hobbes says, "if any two men desire the same thing, which nevertheless they cannot both enjoy, they become enemies; and in the way to the End...endever to destroy or subdue one another." In the natural condition, "the life of man" is "solitary, poore, nasty, brutish and short."[7]

The means by which humans escaped such a condition, as imagined by Hobbes, are nicely characterized by Nisbet: "It will suffice for our purpose here to say only that in time the individual's egoistic desire for his own greatest advantage—that is his instinct for self-preservation—managed somehow to unite with the reason which is native to man and through which even in the presocial state he could presumably foresee the advantages in sovereignty and absolute political association" (SP, 28). The result is a "social contract" in which individuals transfer their natural powers to an absolute sovereign—the great Leviathan—awful enough to ensure that each subject will abide by the contracts he has entered into with others. (As Locke puts it, Hobbes imagines that in order to avoid foxes and polecats men decided to put themselves in the clutches of a lion.[8]) According to Hobbes, "without the terror of some Power" that compels us to observe the laws of justice and equity, our natural passions "carry us to Partiality, Pride, Revenge and the like."[9] For Hobbes, there is no middle ground between the condition of war and the absolute state. Political affirmation indeed.

Concerning Hobbes's "social nihilism," there are no natural social associations, and he firmly restricts extra-political associations within political society. The family, he maintains, is not natural. In the state of nature fathers copulated and then drifted, and mothers had absolute dominion over their children. The "infant is first in the power of the Mother, so she may either nourish it or expose it; if she nourish it, it oweth its life to the mother, and is therefore obliged to obey her...."[10] Conjugal society is maintained only by the force of matrimonial law within political society, and even within political society the family seemingly has no purpose beyond procreation. As Nisbet observes, Hobbes certainly does not see the family "as the true source of man's moral nature, as the model of all forms of association. In Hobbes's system of thought everything proceeds from atomistic individuals, their instincts and reason, and from contractual agreement among them. There is no place for relationships of ascribed, historically given status" (QC, 136).

Hobbes denounces any mixed or divided sovereignty that would represent a plurality of interests, and he sees little need for social groups and associations. Concerning the division of political power into the person of the sovereign and two separate assemblies, he says it would be like a man he once saw "that had a man growing out of his side, with a head, arms, breast, and stomach of his own: If he had had another man growing out of his other side, the comparison might then be exact."[11] Similarly, he calls the "immoderate greatnesse of a town"[12] a terrible infirmity and laments the existence of corporations, "which are as it were many lesser Commonwealths in the bowels of a greater, like worms in the entrayles of a naturall man."[13] Elsewhere, Hobbes states his suspicions of universities and decries with equal vigor the "leagues" of great families and Corporations of Beggars, Thieves and Gypsies.[14] "But," as Nisbet notes, "of all associations, it is the Church that Hobbes fears most. By reason of its tenacious hold upon men's spiritual allegiances, the Church will always be a divisive force within the commonwealth unless it is made strictly subordinate to the political power" (QC, 136). Which is, needless to say, precisely what Hobbes proposed.

As Nisbet observes, despite Hobbes's severe views toward social associations, the power of the state was not for him an end in itself. Hobbes's ideal state is meant to serve the individual. "Hobbes did not seek the extermination of individual rights but their fulfillment. This could be accomplished only by removing social barriers to individual autonomy. In his eyes the greatest claim of the absolute State lay in its power to create an environment for the individual's pursuit of his natural ends" (QC, 137-138).

The individual and the state figure prominently in Rousseau's thought as well. Indeed, Rousseau's work depicts radical individualism, contempt for society, and adulation for the state in their purest forms. He takes political affirmation and social nihilism to new heights. Nisbet observes, "Rousseau sees the State as the most exalted of all forms of moral community. For Rousseau there is no morality, no freedom, no community outside the structure of the State." Moreover, "Rousseau is the first of the modern philosophers to see in the State a means of resolving the conflicts, not merely among institutions, but within the individual himself" (QC, 140). In Rousseau's eyes, these individual conflicts stem from society, and the "State is the means by which the individual can be freed of the restrictive tyrannies that compose society" (QC, 143). For these reasons, Nisbet, in an early letter to Russell Kirk, called Rousseau "the real demon of the modern mind."

The intellectual crux of Rousseau's thought lies in his moral psychology, his view of the relationship between the self and society. In *Emile,* he asserts that by nature humans possess self-love, *amour de soi*, which is "always good and always in conformity with order."[15] He then proclaims: "Let us set down as an incontestable maxim that the first movements of nature are always right. There is no original perversity in the human heart. There is not a single vice to be found in it of which it can not be said how and once it entered."[16] But reason, imagination, and the "sentiment of his connections" with others create within man the possibility of a transformed and perverted form of self-love that depends upon social comparison—*amour-propre*. "Self-love which regards only ourselves is contented when our true needs are satisfied. But *amour-propre*, which makes comparisons, is never content, and never could be, because this sentiment, preferring ourselves to others, also demands others to prefer us to themselves, which is impossible."[17] For Rousseau, the desire for recognition and praise creates perversities in the human heart—jealousy, envy, imperiousness, vindictiveness, competitiveness, and deceit. What was whole and satisfied becomes divided and vicious. Rousseau thus believes that attention to others does not lead to healthy moral regulation. Rather, it causes inauthentic dependency upon "opinion" and fosters invidious distinctions. In short, the several institutions of society are sources of vice, not virtue, for Rousseau, and, as Nisbet says, "like Plato, Rousseau saw the political community, absolute, indivisible and omnipotent, as the only possible haven from the ills and torments of society" (SP, 37).

According to Rousseau, *amour-propre* did not exist in the state of nature. In nature humans enjoyed simple and undivided *amour de soi,* and the natural sentiment of pity took "the place of laws, mores and virtues."[18] *Amour-propre* arose only with civil society, and the history of civil society was largely a history of the enlargement of *amour-propre* within the human heart. According to *The Discourse on Inequality,* "The first person, who having enclosed a plot of land, took it into his head to say this is mine and found people simple enough to believe him, was the true founder of civil society."[19] This "revolution" ushered in civil society's "tribal" stage, a stage in which the faculties of reason, language, and *amour-propre* were first developed. Although "bloodthirsty and cruel," this was "the happiest and most durable epoch." In it, humans maintained "a middle position between the indolence of our primitive state and the petulant activity of our egocentricity (*amour-propre*), and as long as they applied themselves exclusively to tasks that a single individual could do and to the arts that did not require the cooperation of several hands, they lived as free, healthy, good and happy as they could in accordance with their nature."[20] But, Rousseau continued, the inventions of metallurgy and agriculture replaced this happy state with one in which men needed one another, inequality was heightened, and *amour-propre* "nearly reached the limit of the perfection of which it is capable."[21] And, alas, in their further progress, things only worsened. "Luxury, impossible to prevent among men who are greedy for their own conveniences and for the esteem of others, soon completes the evil that societies have begun.... From society and the luxury it engenders, arise the liberal and mechanical arts, commerce, letters and all those useless things that make industry flourish, enriching and ruining states."[22] Indeed, luxury is "the worst of all evils in any state," and, for Rousseau, the supposed progress of civil society is in actuality "the decay of the species."[23]

This decay, however, did not unfold uninterrupted. Rousseau's contemporaries, such as David Hume, denounced the classical republicanism of early Rome and Sparta—not the least because the commercial indolence of these cities led to slavery—but Rousseau saw in Rome, and especially in Sparta, the heights of human achievement. Regarding the latter, he says in *The Discourse on the Sciences and the Arts*, "Could I forget that it was in the very bosom of Greece that there was seen to arise that city as famous for her happy ignorance as for the wisdom of her laws, that republic of demi-gods rather than men, so superior to humanity did their virtues seem? O Sparta!"[24] Rousseau peceived in Sparta the closest real approximation to his ideal society—a society whose size was "limited by the extent of human faculties," where a person's affections were to the homeland rather than to the land, and where *amour-propre* became expressions of patriotic and martial virtue. In Sparta, men were true *citizens* and patriots.

In modern civil society, by contrast, men were mere *bourgeois*. "The bourgeois," in the words of one commentator, is Rousseau's "great invention."[25] The bourgeois, for Rousseau, "is unpoetic, unerotic, unheroic, neither aristocrat nor of the people; he is not a citizen, and his religion is pallid and this-worldly."[26] While Rousseau's contemporaries trained their eyes on the *ancien régime*, Rousseau knew the *ancien régime* was on its "last legs" and heaped his scorn on the emerging bourgeois order.[27] Nonetheless, Rousseau saw that we could not literally go back to our natural condition or to the age of tribes and city-states in order to remedy the problems of bourgeois society. Consequently, "He who dares to undertake the establishment of a people should feel that he is, so to speak, in a position to change human nature, to transform each individual (who by himself is a perfect and solitary whole) into a part of a larger whole from which this individual receives, in a sense, his life and being."[28] According to *The Social Contract*, the solution to the problem of modern civil society was a state guided by a legislator capable of fusing particular wills into a "general will." Thus, we have what Pierre Manent calls Rousseau's paradox: "On the one hand, society is essentially contrary to nature; on the other, it comes nearer to conforming to nature only insofar as it imposes the greatest unity possible on its members, identifying with everyone and the whole—in short, only insofar as it changes man's nature."[29] The solution to the problem of society is a political community of unprecedented extent and powers. In Nisbet's words, for Rousseau, the "individual lives a free life within the frame of his complete surrender to the omnipotent state. The state is the liberator of the individual from the toils of society" (SP, 41).

Although the extreme individualism of *The Discourses* and the collectivism of *The Social Contract* have sometimes perplexed readers, these works do form a whole: together they exhibit a thoroughgoing disdain for the pluralism, spontaneity, interdependency, and independence of the communities and institutions of society. For Rousseau, society splinters and fragments the elementary and unified soul of natural man, the modern remedy for which is the general will. Certainly, the practical implications of Rousseau's doctrine of the general will are many, but Nisbet cites Rousseau's discussion of "civil religion" in the final chapter of *The Social Contract* as most typical (SP, 44). This discussion, Nisbet says, displays Rousseau's disdain for the Christian church while revealing that "it is the essential humanity in the Christian faith that Rousseau despises" (SP, 45).

Specifically, Rousseau proposed a unified and authoritarian state religion as an essential alternative to divisive Roman Catholicism and to the weakness of what he called "True Christianity." Roman Catholicism, for Rousseau, was "bizarre," hardly worth the efforts to prove its faults. Because it existed independently of the state, Rousseau said, it "gives men two sets of legislation, two leaders, and two homelands," thereby subjecting them "to contradictory duties" and preventing them "from being simultaneously devout men and citizens."[30] True Christianity is a religion of the heart, without rites or a homeland, but "Christianity preaches servitude and dependence.... True Christians are made to be slaves."[31] What is needed, therefore, "is a purely civil profession of faith, the articles of which it belongs to the sovereign to establish, not exactly as dogmas of religion, but as sentiments of sociability, without which it is impossible to be a good citizen or a faithful subject."[32] These dogmas should be simple—the existence of God and an afterlife, "the happiness of the just; the punishment of the wicked; the sanctity of the social contract and the laws"—and it is the sovereign's duty "to banish anyone who does not believe" these dogmas.[33] Cults and intolerance cannot be tolerated, Rousseau says. Nothing should compete with the sovereignty of the state.

The influence here of Machiavelli's view of Christianity and republican virtue is clear. Yet, Rousseau says:

> Of all the Christian writers, the philosopher Hobbes is the only one who clearly saw the evil and the remedy, who dared to propose the unification of the two heads of the eagle and the complete restoration of political unity, without which no state or government will ever be well constituted. But he should have seen that the dominating spirit of Christianity was incompatible with his system, and that the interest of the priest would always be stronger than that of the state. It is not so much what is horrible and false in his political theory as what is just and true that has caused it to be hated.[34]

On certain points Hobbes and Rousseau are very different: for example, the vile human nature that Hobbes attributes to base natural propensities and passions, Rousseau sees as the exclusive product of society. Yet, Nisbet observes (SP, 35-36), both share contempt for those social institutions that are independent of state power, and, in the end, their political visions converge: both imagine an ideal commonwealth containing individuals and the state, without communities or intermediate associations to mediate between them.

Pluralism

Monism, Nisbet says, has been rising in the modern era, especially in its many Rousseauian forms. Yet social pluralism, which emphasizes the small and parochial forms of allegiance and authority, has been far from moribund. Social pluralists, he observes, have consistently maintained that communal associations are essential to freedom, individuality, and even to love of the larger community, and they have contended against arbitrary and bureaucratic state power. Indeed, according to Nisbet, the intellectual sources of social pluralism are many and quite varied. They range from Burkean conservatism to the nineteenth-century liberalism of Acton and Tocqueville to the anarchist mutualism of Lammenais, Proudhon, and Kropotkin. Nisbet treats at length each of these thinkers and for each—including the radical anarchists—he has profound intellectual admiration. But I will limit myself here to commenting on Nisbet's two greatest intellectual heroes—Burke and Tocqueville.

Modern social pluralism, Nisbet says, originated "pretty much in Burke's *Reflections on the Revolution in France.*" As Nisbet immediately notes, "Burke, it is useful to remember, had given his endorsement to four revolutions—English, American, Indian and Irish—which is a good record for any liberal or radical, much less one who has come to be known as the father of conservatism" (MMS, 138). His response to the French Revolution, Nisbet asserts, was not a departure from his earlier principles but, rather, a consistent denunciation of arbitrary power. "His attack on the French Revolution sprang from precisely those principles that had underlain his defense of the American colonists and the people of India. These principles were rooted in Burke's profound belief in the superiority of traditional society and its component groups and associations, as well as what he regarded as its inherent organic processes of change, over centralized political power...." (SP, 53).

In the course of his attack on the French Revolution, Burke attacked its premises which, like the Jacobins themselves, he saw as Rousseauian. Burke was as fervent in his disdain for Rousseau as he was for the revolutionaries. He called Rousseau "the philosopher of vanity," "the insane Socrates of the National Assembly," and the "wild, ferocious, low-minded, hard-hearted father of the Revolution."[35] Similarly, he characterized the revolutionaries as "literary caballers," "intriguing philosophers," "political theologians," and "physicians of the state."[36] Indeed, Burke's attacks on the revolutionaries melded with his attacks on Rousseau because Burke believed Rousseau was the "model" or "moral hero" of the revolutionaries. "Everybody knows that there is a great dispute amongst their leaders, which of them is the best resemblance to Rousseau."[37] To be sure, what separates Burke from Rousseau involves more than their very different views of sovereignty and society, but it is the stark antithesis of political monism and social pluralism that is at the center of most other differences between these two thinkers. Concerning the origins of this antithesis, Nisbet says, "It is fitting that we know Burke to have been a deep admirer of Aristotle as we do Rousseau to have been an equally ardent admirer of Plato" (SP, 50).

Whereas Rousseau claimed that man is by nature good and corrupted by artificial society, Burke believed that "Art is man's nature. We are as much, at least, in a state of nature in formed manhood, as in immature and helpless infancy."[38] Man is not man without the social order. As Nisbet observes, "Burke has scant use for any view of man's nature that sees the basis of order, freedom or even individuality in the highest sense of the term, to lie in man as a biologically created being. The basis of all these is inseparable from civil society, from the fabric of community" (SP, 54-55). Thus, although Burke maintained a version of natural law, he was extremely wary of those who invoked an "all-atoning" natural right of liberty. Burke cherished liberty but he saw that it resulted more from convention and artful reason than from nature. Without wisdom and virtue, he said, liberty "is the greatest of all possible evils; for it is folly, vice and madness without tuition or restraint."[39] Liberty and restraint must be combined; free government "requires much thought, deep reflection, a sagacious, powerful and combining mind."[40]

Employing the simplifying metaphysic supplied by Rousseau, the revolutionaries attempted to draw authority to Paris, while other divisions of the kingdom were "hacked and torn to pieces," separated "from all their habitual means, and even principles of union."[41] Thus, concerning the revolutionaries' scheme to redraw districts according to population size and geometric symmetry in order that "all local ideas should be shrunk, and that the people should no longer be Gascons, Picards, Bretons, Normans, but Frenchmen," Burke says that instead of being Frenchmen with one country and one heart, the people "will shortly have no country. No man ever was attached by a sense of pride, partiality, or real affection, to a description of square measurement.... We begin our public affections in our families. No cold relation is a zealous citizen. We pass on to our neighborhoods, and our habitual provincial connections. These are inns and resting places....The love of the whole is not extinguished by this subordinate partiality."[42] The love of the whole *depends* upon this subordinate partiality (PS, 58).

As Burke put it early in the *Reflections,* "To be attached to the subdivision, to love the little platoon we belong to in society, is the first principle (the germ as it were) of public affections."[43] And later on, "The municipal corporations of the universal kingdom are not morally at liberty at their pleasure, and on the speculations of a contingent improvement, wholly to separate and tear asunder the bands of subordinate community."[44] To do so is to "dissolve it into an unsocial, uncivil, unconnected chaos of elementary principles." The ultimate consequence of the French Revolution, unlike the Whig Revolution of 1688, Burke states, was to create "the organic moleculae of a disbanded people." To disband the little platoon is to foster "weakness, disconnection and confusion."[45] To cast away the "coat of prejudice," which "renders man's virtue habit," leaves individuals with nothing but naked reason, "skeptical and puzzled," unable to act in moments of decision.[46] According to Nisbet, it was the "rationalist simplicity" of the French revolutionaries that Burke feared and despised most because of its destructive effects upon the plural social order (SP, 56). Without tradition and mediating institutions, we have, Burke said, what Tocqueville would later call "individualism."

Another consequence of the eradication of prejudice and particularistic affections Burke observed among the revolutionaries was a "new-invented virtue"—universal benevolence. This virtue combines universal reason with native affection, creating a love of humanity that is indifferent to particular people. This virtue, the "moral hero" of the revolution displayed in abundance, according to Burke. Rousseau, who turned over each of his five illegitimate children to a state-run foundling home, exhibited constantly "the stores of his powerful rhetoric in the expression of universal benevolence, whilst his heart was incapable of harboring one spark of common parental affection.... He melts with tenderness for those only who touch him by the remotest relation, and then, without one natural pang, casts away, as a sort of offal and excrement, the spawn of his disgustful amours and sends his children to the hospital of foundlings."[47] Nisbet records that Rousseau justified his treatment of his children by claiming adherence to Plato's idea of true citizenship (SP, 37).

Burke displayed unparalleled prescience in 1790 regarding the ultimate conclusion of the French Revolution. He said, "the government, be it what it may, will immediately degenerate into a military democracy; a species of political monster, which has always ended by devouring those who have produced it."[48]

Tocqueville, writing fifty years after Burke, knew all too well, of course, about this political monster and how it went about devouring those who produced it. Tocqueville labored in both *The Old Regime and the French Revolution* and *Democracy in America* to comprehend the enduring social and political results of the French Revolution. And, as Nisbet observes, "There is a clear and logical line of descent from Burke's espousal of traditional groups and associations, his belief in limits on all forms of power, and his advocacy of traditionalist pluralism and of decentralization to the fundamental principles in Tocqueville's classic *Democracy in America*...." (SP, 58). In fact, Nisbet says, "we may justly say that through Tocqueville the seminal ideas of Aristotle and then of Burke were brought into unique focus for the twentieth century" (SP, 68).

"Tocqueville's central thesis" in *Democracy in America*, Nisbet says, "can be stated simply. All that alienates man in modern society from traditional authority—from class, guild, church and so on—tends to drive him ever more forcefully into the haven of power, power conceived not as something remote and fearful but as close, sealing, intimate and providential: the power, that is, of modern democracy with its roots in public opinion" (ST, 120). Unlike the conservatives of his day, Tocqueville did not seek to combat democracy. The era launched by the American Revolution and especially by the French Revolution spelled for Tocqueville the inevitable spread of democracy. Tocqueville's concern was to comprehend the contexts in which liberty could be preserved within democratic times and places.

Alas, democracy does not typically inspire the greatest passion for liberty, but rather for equality. And the spirit of equality, Tocqueville said, fosters "individualism," the tendency to isolate oneself with one's family and friends with no civic concern beyond this small circle. Individualism, Tocqueville believed, creates a void filled by a centralized authority that enervates and stifles initiative. Thus, democracy tends toward a type of "despotism" quite different from past forms of tyranny. In Tocqueville's words: "Above this race of men stands an immense and tutelary power, which takes upon itself alone to secure their gratifications and to watch over their fate. That power is absolute, minute, regular, provident and mild. It would be like the authority of a parent if, like that authority, its object was to prepare men for manhood; but it seeks, on the contrary, to keep them in perpetual childhood...."[49]

Tocqueville did not believe that "democratic despotism" was inevitable, although he did think that the tendency toward despotism was inherent in democracy. In fact, although he saw much during his 1831 visit to the United States that was disconcerting—especially American restlessness and materialism—he also found evidence of conditions wherein democracy coexisted with liberty. Indeed, he believed, that the American experience could instruct Europeans and especially the French— whose experience with democracy had been so disastrous—as to what conditions were necessary to forestall individualism and democratic despotism. Nisbet records that Tocqueville's appreciation for American institutions was deep enough that when he wrote the preface to the twelfth French edition of *Democracy in America,* just after the turbulent events of 1848, he declared that any republic worthy of the name must be based upon American principles (MMS, 154). Specifically, according to Nisbet's enumeration, Tocqueville identified five conditions he believed were necessary for the preservation of liberty within democratic societies, each of which he considered to be present in Jacksonian America.

Nisbet writes that "Fundamental among the causes of continued freedom in American democracy, Tocqueville shows us, is the American principle of division of authority in society." In America, individual rights were obtained through diversification of authority, Tocqueville believed, and this "principle underlies...not merely the overall structure of authority in America but also each of the several major institutions in American life, including religion, economy and political government itself " (SP, 65).

A second source of freedom in the United States, according to Tocqueville, was the presence and appeal of local institutions. This, for Tocqueville, was very important, for, "How can a populace unaccustomed to freedom in small concerns learn to use it temperately in great affairs?" Local institutions were schoolhouses of citizenship and liberty.

A third cause of American freedom was the American federal system, which separated the executive, judicial, and legislative branches of the national government from each other and separated the powers of the national government from state and local powers. The American federal system was designed not to consolidate authority absolutely within one person or assembly, as Hobbes and Rousseau advocated, but rather to divide and disperse sovereignty such that ambition could battle with ambition.

Fourth among the conditions of liberty was freedom of the press. The American free press was important for a number of reasons, Tocqueville thought, not the least of which was that, whereas in nineteenth-century England notables could accomplish great ends and in France the people were likely to appeal to the government when great issues arose, in America spontaneous associations emerged in order to address pressing needs and undertake great tasks. A free press was essential for an idea to be planted in enough minds for people to form associations of sufficient size to address important causes.

Fifth among the conditions of freedom was freedom of association. This was extraordinarily important to Tocqueville, who was struck both by the number of civil and political associations in America and by their enormous vitality. These associations were essential to overcome the inherent weakness of individuals within democracy and to defend against the centralization of power. In short, voluntary associations simultaneously combated the twin evils of individualism and democratic despotism.

In *The Social Philosophers,* Nisbet asserts, "Of all in Western thought who have addressed themselves to the problem of liberty, it is Tocqueville who seems to speak most eloquently and forcefully to the democracies of the twentieth century" (SP, 68). Tocqueville makes the ideas of social pluralism stretching back to Aristotle pertinent to contemporary democratic societies. Tocqueville, Nisbet maintained, skillfully described both the dangers we face and the avenues that must be taken to avoid them. Liberty, of course, has indeed been eroded in the manner that Tocqueville imagined it might, said Nisbet, chiefly as a consequence of war and its equivalents—depression, poverty, and the like. Yet, according to Nisbet, the ways to maintain or recover liberty described by Tocqueville and other social pluralists are as instructive today as Tocqueville hoped they might be to his contemporary countrymen and other Europeans.

The final chapter of this book argues that the eighteenth-century classical liberal tradition was an additional, and very important, source of social pluralism about which Nisbet was mostly silent. In fact, certain of the classical liberals—David Hume and Adam Smith, for example—defended local and parochial institutions especially well because, like Burke, they consistently maintained that such institutions arise from specific and innate, natural sentiments—from human nature. Nisbet sometimes also refers to human nature, but in his direct commentaries on contemporary life, he typically defends intermediate institutions in terms of their functionality, efficiency, and efficacy. Although such terms are largely reliable and illuminating, without a consistent and bedrock standard—divine or natural—by which to make judgments, Nisbet is led, I believe, to an occasional faulty conclusion. For example, he cited the youth communes of the 1970s as indicating the recovery of community (1974, 28), and he was friendly toward Durkheim's "corporatism," a scheme by which professions and industries would be arranged on communal principles (SED, 136-145). But neither communes nor corporatism conforms with the natural sentiments as described by the classical liberals or Burke. This, though, is not the place to dwell on such a minor failing, for

Nisbet is one of postwar America's most important social pluralists, and there is no doubt that he was correct in believing that the tradition of social pluralism, not that of political monism, "is by far the more relevant to the needs of our time." He acknowledged that in some ages and societies, a measure of political affirmation was needed, but "we live nevertheless in a time of saturation of social order by political power," a time hungry for the rejuvenation of the tradition of social pluralism (TA, 246).

CONSERVATIVE DOGMATICS

ACCORDING TO NISBET, he did not write *The Quest for Community* "as a conservative book" (C, 97). His research for the book over the previous fifteen years had led him to think of conservatism as a European way of thinking associated especially with reaction to the French Revolution. Whatever sympathies he may have had with conservatism before 1953, Nisbet held to a version of the thesis, developed explicitly by Louis Hartz in 1955, that liberalism was the only authentic American political and intellectual tradition.[1] Certainly, he did not believe that defense of business and opposition to the New Deal alone qualified one as a conservative.

Nisbet's view began to change in 1953 due largely to his encounter with Russell Kirk's *The Conservative Mind*. This book, Nisbet says, "gave scholarly and timely pedigree to conservatism in England and the United States, demonstrating the key role of

Burke in both countries" (c, 97). Nisbet began to recognize and write about a genuine conservative American tradition, with both European and indigenous roots. In 1976, for example, he penned an essay titled "The Social Impact of the American Revolution" in which he investigated the moderate and conservative nature of the American Revolution. He described the revolution as unique because of "the absence of the kind of passion, zeal and millennialist conviction that in other countries produced terror and left a heritage of bitterness lasting to the present day." He attributed these subdued tendencies to the dispersal of power; the strong presence of religion; the existence of intermediate, voluntary, and autonomous associations; and to the American class structure, which prevented "any class from becoming forever identified with a political position rising from the Revolution" (MMS, 178, 180-192). In Nisbet's eyes, American soil ultimately proved to be very fertile for conservative ideas. In *Prejudices: A Philosophical Dictionary,* published in 1982, he claimed that there have been "two significant eruptions of conservative ideology in modern Western thought: first in 1790-1810 in Western Europe chiefly, but to some degree in the United States; and then in 1950-1970, largely in America" (P, 55).

Both of these eruptions, Nisbet says, were triggered by the state extending itself "ever more rapaciously" into traditional society, and in each Burke figured prominently. Burke initiated the first eruption, and "it was in substantial degree a revival of the study of Burke in the mid-twentieth century that furnished the stuff of the second eruption" (p, 55). Most of what today is regarded as philosophical conservatism derives from the principles announced by Burke in his denunciation of the French Revolution. Burke was immediately followed by Bonald and de Maistre in France, Coleridge and Southey in England, Savigny and Hegel in Germany, Haller in Switzerland, and Balmes in Spain; and although the second eruption produced no de Maistre or Hegel, the American conservatives of the 1950s and 1960s—Mises, Hayek, Kirk, Weaver, Buckley, Kristol, among others—saw themselves in much the same position as had Burke and his fellow conservatives in the aftermath of the French Revolution. "Ever since the New Deal, American thought had been governed in extraordinary measure by the Gods of political centralization, collectivism, central planning and devotion to the national state over traditional society. Like Burke, the new conservatives called attention to the values of localism and regionalism, religion, patriotism, and political decentralization" (p, 58).

Needless to say, Nisbet himself must be counted among those who contributed most to the conservative renascence of the 1950s and 1960s. Nisbet is well described as the most prominent and influential conservative sociologist in postwar America. But he was also one of America's foremost sociologists of conservatism because several of his writings analyze conservatism as a social and intellectual movement. Most important and most obvious in this regard is *Conservatism: Dream and Reality*. Published in 1986, this book analyzes what Nisbet calls the "dogmatics" of conservatism, where "dogmatics" are the "more or less coherent and persistent bodies of belief and value which have determinative influence upon at least a part of their holders' lives." Like theology, dogmatics "relate to the individual's proper place under a system of authority, divine or secular" (c, 21). Nisbet's approach to conservative dogmatics is not historical but what he calls an "anatomy" of conservatism. This approach is possible, he says, because the major themes of conservatism have as much currency today as they did a century or two ago. The dogmatics of conservatism are singular among the salient beliefs of the different modern political perspectives. Their continuity and consistency extend over the past two hundred years. These dogmatics, as identified in *Conservatism*, are taken up in this chapter, although much of the content is drawn from other writings by Nisbet.

History and Tradition

Over the past two hundred years, conservatism has been one of the three chief social and political perspectives in the West, the other two being liberalism and socialism. Although these three are commonly distinguished by their differing conceptions of the individual and the state, Nisbet argues that a more useful approach adds the factor of groups or associations that mediate between the individual and the state. Concerning the triangular relationship of the individual, the social group, and the state, conservatism and socialism are opposite extremes. Whereas conservatism "took to its bosom the rights of church, social class, family and property," socialism had virtually no regard for the traditional rights of intermediate groups. "Liberalism," Nisbet says, "falls about half way" between conservatism and socialism. Although the liberalism of Bentham and Mill reveals "overriding sympathies with the individual and his rights against the state and the social groups alike," Tocqueville's impression upon Mill, Nisbet observes, produced "an indulgence in certain areas of liberal thought for groups, especially voluntary associations, that adds up to a liberal pluralism" (C, 22).

The differences among the three modern political perspectives, Nisbet says, can be accounted for largely by their different views of history and tradition. Whereas progressivists and socialists believe that society is best constituted by rational forethought, planning, and design, conservatives believe that society and social change are organic in nature. Conservatives see society as evolving over time, and they believe that the elements that form the tissue of society—the beliefs, mores, and institutions—are interrelated and interdependent. In the conservative view, the past, the present, and the future are necessarily linked, and this linkage is strongest and most firm when the past is viewed as a repository of concrete experience, practical wisdom, and rough guides to action. How things have come to be the way they are is simply beyond the rational comprehension of any individual or set of individuals. Institutions and practices can and often do serve functions and fulfill needs that are time-tested, but they cannot be identified and appreciated by individual, hubristic reason. Given these features, Nisbet believes that "efforts, however well-intentioned, to reform or remake one part of society inevitably violate the complex lines of relationship which exist and must exist in any stable society" (1952, 170).

This is not to say that conservatives oppose all change. In this regard, Nisbet reminds us of Burke's famous observation: "A state without the means of some change is without the means of its conservation" (c, 26). What Burke and other conservatives oppose is what Burke called the "spirit of innovation," a uniform disdain for the past and a belief in change for its own sake. Such a view of the past, Nisbet says, is farcical because history "has been very much the kind of force that natural selection is for the biological evolutionist." History is an operation of chance and selection. "There is ingrained in evolutionary selection a wisdom astronomically superior to any wisdom imaginable in a man" (c, 28).[2] Thus, in the conservative view, "the real constitution of a people lies in the history of its institutions, not in a piece of paper…" (c, 27). The spontaneous order of customs and tradition provides stability and a mechanism for change far superior to proclamations, declarations, and schemes of improvement.

Prejudice and Reason

In the conservative view, the great prejudice of the Enlightenment was the prejudice against prejudice. The Enlightenment insisted that all things be brought for judgment to the bar of reason; no prejudice was seen as legitimate. Nisbet, however, says that "There is in prejudice an indwelling wisdom that is the product of the centuries and of man's deep needs for security" (1952, 170). Although prejudice is the object of rationalist contempt, it charts courses of action that do not bedazzle the individual nor render him incapable of decision by every circumstance that arises. Prerational, emotional attachment to certain habits, beliefs, and practices contributes to an understanding of the world that is prerequisite to action; and, as Nisbet notes, this mode of understanding or knowledge is the very stuff of common sense or *sensus communis*. "[I]t is knowledge that is *common* among individuals in a nation, not something that is the special preserve of an intellectual elite" (c, 30). "At stake in the conservative appeal to prejudice in human behavior is a whole type of knowledge" according to Nisbet. "It is the kind of knowledge that William James described as 'knowledge of' in contrast to 'knowledge about'" (c, 31). The essence of the first type of knowledge is its practicality. It derives directly from experience, through experiment and trial and error. It is vivid and immediate. By contrast, the second type of knowledge is mediated: it is acquired "from a textbook, from learning *about* something that can be presented in the form of abstract or general principle, something that is susceptible to prescriptive formulae, and is at its most resplendent when it can be set forth in logical fashion" (c, 32).

This distinction between two types of knowledge, Nisbet says, has been fundamental to conservative criticisms "of all political utopianism and a great deal of political reform." The utopian and reformer are more likely to be animated by abstract principle than a sense of expediency and practicality gained through concrete experience. The differences between these two types of knowledge formed the basis of Aristotle's critique of Plato. Against the theoretical musings of Plato's pure reason, Aristotle asserted the importance of *phronesis* or practical wisdom. Similarly and more recently, Michael Oakeshott has criticized political reformers for their "knowledge of technique" and their lack of "practical knowledge." In fact, according to Oakeshott, from the reformist point of view, practical knowledge is not knowledge at all. There is no knowledge that is not technical knowledge—"thus," Nisbet says, "the source of the familiar wail in human history that governments be in the hands of engineers, technocrats and other academic specialists." Wherever the rationalist mind has flourished, the dream has been of "either a single great intelligence or some small class of intelligences" to rule and to be "rid once and for all of the kinds of government which are formed upon mere use and wont, habit, custom and tradition, and upon representative bodies, semi-public commissions and other bodies, judicial buffers, and other restraints upon pure deductive reason" (C, 32-33).

Authority and Power

The rationalist admires the uniformity and homogeneity of power but dismisses the virtues of traditional intermediate social groups. The conservative, on the other hand, embraces the principle of the legitimacy of authority, which is necessary to preserving local and parochial institutions. As Nisbet says, "Authority is legitimate when it proceeds from the customs and traditions of a people, when it is formed by innumerable links in a chain that begins with the family, rises through community and class, and culminates in the larger society" (1952, 172). Concern for the larger society, in the conservative view, is not in conflict with the smaller patriotisms of life. Larger concerns rely upon the particularism and legitimate authority of subordinate groups. As Alexander Pope put it in "An Essay on Man":

> God loves from the Whole to Parts: but human soul
> Must rise from Individual to the Whole.
> Self-Love but serves the virtuous mind to wake,
> As the small pebble stirs the peaceful lake;
> The centre mov'd, a circle strait succeeds,
> Another still, and still another spreads,
> Friend, parent, neighbor, first it will embrace,
> His country next, and next all human race....[3]

In addition to instilling the smaller allegiances required for larger allegiances, subordinate, intermediate groups offer the first requisite of social order—self-restraint. External, distant, and coercive power cannot accomplish this all-important task. This arises from the obligations, loyalties, and authority from within the innermost circles of our social lives. To be freed from these social circles is no freedom at all. As Burke observed, when individuals are separated from traditional ties "and have got themselves loose, not from restraint, but from the protection of all the principles of natural authority and legitimate subordination, they become the natural prey of imposters...." (quoted in 1952, 170). As Nisbet says, the "loose individual" becomes an isolated atom within the masses, "an aggregate discernable less by numbers than its lack of internal social structure, integrating tradition and shared moral values" (c, 45); and, as conservatives such as Burke, Ortega y Gasset, and Burkhardt, among others, all observed, a mass society of desocialized individuals is susceptible to political charlatans.

"Let it not, though, be thought that conservatives have been or are in favor of a weak central government. Far from it," Nisbet says (c, 41). Extensive administration and arbitrary power, both of which conservatives fear, should not be confused with a strong and energetic government. The latter is as important to ordered liberty as the former are dangerous. Government of settled law and sure punishment for transgression of the law is essential to civil and public order. Without it there can be no spontaneous sociability. "But," Nisbet says "from centrality of government it does not follow that it must be omnicompetent, responsible for daily existence, and ever in our lives, and, worst of all, pretend moral teacher, guide to virtue, and mother of spirit" (C, 42).

Liberty and Equality

"There is no principle more basic in the conservative philosophy," Nisbet says, "than that of the inherent and absolute incompatibility between liberty and equality" (C, 47). This is because the two ends necessarily conflict. Freedom thrives, says Nisbet, "in cultural diversity, in local and regional differentiation, in associative pluralism, and, above all, in diversification of power" (QC, 265). The purpose of freedom or liberty is to protect individual and family property, both material and immaterial. "The inherent objective of equality, on the other hand, is that of some kind of redistribution or leveling of the unequally shared material and immaterial values of a community" (C, 47). Instead of diversified authority, equality demands consolidated and uniform power.

This difference, Nisbet says, can be thought of as two very different and typically incompatible views of freedom: "freedom from," the object of conservative adulation, and "freedom to," the chief aim of egalitarianism (C, 48). Although Nisbet does not mention him by name, Sir Isaiah Berlin most fully developed this distinction. The first form of liberty Berlin calls "negative" liberty. It exists to the degree that a person is free from interference from others in the pursuit of his or her activities. Berlin says, "The defense of liberty consists in the 'negative' goal of warding off interference."[4] The second concept of liberty, what Berlin calls "positive" liberty, rests upon a particular psychology developed first by Rousseau. This psychology asserts the existence of, first, an empirical self and, second, a "real" ideal self aching for liberation from the confines of nature or "spiritual slavery." "Presently," Berlin says, "the two selves may be represented by an even larger gap: the real self may be conceived as something wider than the individual, as a social whole of which the individual is an element or aspect.... This entity is then identified as being the 'true' self which, by imposing its collective, or 'organic' single will upon its recalcitrant 'members,' achieves its own, and therefore their, 'higher' freedom."[5] According to "positive" liberty, men must be coerced in order to be free because they are blind, ignorant, avaricious, or otherwise corrupt.

Equality is both a means to an end and an end in itself, within the concept of positive liberty. It is the means by which differences among individuals can be leveled, making them more likely to identify their "true" selves in the collective; it is worthwhile in itself because inequality wounds the esteem of those of lesser endowments. Positive liberty, Berlin says, inevitably leads to the demand to be liberated from social dependency. Berlin continues. "What I demand is an alteration of the attitude toward me of those whose opinions and behavior help to determine my own image of myself."[6]

Positive liberty is anathema to conservatives. Nisbet says, "Social differentiation, hierarchy and functional rather than mechanical consensus are as vital to freedom as to order. This is the nub of the conservative philosophy of freedom and equality." Other than legal and constitutional equality, all other forms of equality "seem to the conservative to threaten the liberties of both individual and group, liberties which are inseparable from the built-in differentiation, variety, and variable opportunity that are so often the target of the equalizer" (c, 51). For example, it is no accident that conservatives venerate the family while egalitarians are often, quite simply, family haters. Differentiation, variety, and fluid opportunity are built into the institution of the family. Egalitarians are quite correct when they observe that family circumstances create an advantage for some children relative to other children. What conservatives stress, though, is that this is more a matter of cultural inheritance than of biological inheritance or the inheritance of property. Consequently, no amount of redistribution of property will improve the circumstances of culturally disadvantaged children. Burke observed, "Those who attempt to level, never equalize" (quoted in c, 51).

This is not to say that conservatives are or should be indifferent to the plight of the truly disadvantaged.[7] Nisbet believes that the conservative argument on this is easily stated: "There are groups beginning with the family and including the neighborhood and church, which are duly constituted to render assistance and in the form of mutual-aid, not high-flown charity from a bureaucracy." Nisbet continues, "The primary purpose of government is to look to the conditions of strength of these groups, inasmuch as they are by virtue of age of historical development the best fitted to deal with the majority of problems in individuals' lives" (c, 61-62).

Religion and Morals

Of the three modern political philosophies, conservatism is unique "in its emphasis upon church and the Judaeo-Christian morality" (c, 68). Nisbet records, for example, that Burke takes up more pages in *Reflections on the French Revolution* on the vital role of religion in fostering ordered liberty than on any other topic with the exception of property. But Nisbet quickly notes, "It is the institutional aspect of religion that is alone germane here to political conservatism," because personal religious devotion is not greater among conservatives than among liberals. Nisbet observes that Burke, Bonald, de Maistre, and Disraeli were each tepid in their religious beliefs, as were many early-twentieth-century American conservatives (c, 71-73). But he asserts that personal devotion is not needed to recognize the salutary effect of institutional religion upon the manners and morals of a people. Indeed, as Tocqueville observed, given democracy's natural tendency to foster materialism and self-gratification, the need for institutional religion is greater in democracies than in aristocratic societies. Tocqueville asserted that the doctrine of reincarnation—that the soul of man will pass to the carcass of a hog—is nobler by far than the materialistic doctrine that the soul of man is nothing at all.[8] The bulwark of faith is necessary to ennoble the individual and to enjoin him to higher ends. "The danger of loss of faith in God," G. K. Chesterton affirms, "is not that one will then believe in nothing, but that one will believe in anything" (quoted in c, 73).

A second important institutional function of religion, conservatives believe, is that a strong church can serve as a check upon state power. Indeed, properly balanced, each serves as a restraint upon the other. Thus, Nisbet says, "It is Bonald the political scientist as much as Roman Catholic who divided 'legitimate' society into the three spheres of government, church and family, each destined to be sovereign within its own realm" (c, 71). Among other things, a strong church fosters pluralism and the diversification of power.

According to Nisbet, the focus of conservative writings upon religion entails a distrust of religious enthusiasm. Not one of the "founding fathers of political conservatism," he says, indulged in, or seemed to appreciate, religious zeal. "Religion for them was preeminently public and institutional, something to which loyalty and a decent regard for form were owing, a valuable pillar to both state and society, but not a profound and permeating doctrine, least of all a total experience" (C, 69). "Conservatives," he observes, "have for the most part believed in the Divine much as all educated people believe in gravity or the spherical shape of the earth—firmly but not ecstatically" (C, 74). Accordingly, he concludes in *Prejudices*, whatever else might be said of the millions of Americans who have formed the recent evangelical revival, the term "conservative," in the Burkean sense, cannot be applied to them. "Burke," he notes, "had no use for enthusiasm in either religion or politics, and enthusiasm is what these evangelicals exude." Nisbet does concede that in their devotion to religion, family, and traditional morality, and in their opposition to centralized government and bureaucracy, evangelicals are both sincere and effective. He concludes, therefore, that although they enjoy a prominent place in the political coalition of the contemporary American Right, the status of evangelicals as conservatives is ambiguous at best (P, 59-61).

It should be noted in conclusion that from Nisbet's point of view, the political coalition of the American Right is quite tenuous and not particularly conservative. Evangelicals, in Nisbet's eyes, are at least ambiguous conservatives, but many others on the Right are antipathetic to conservative dogmatics.

These include militarists, libertarian hedonists, those who would use the state to establish a "reign of virtue," advocates of plebiscitary democracy, and populists of every stripe. None of these groups is pursuing what Nisbet called "the sole object of the conservative tradition," which "is the protection of the social order and its constitutive groups from the enveloping bureaucracy of the national state" (P, 59). He conceded, writing in the early 1980s, that current "efforts to reduce the state are like nothing so much as chipmunks trying to bring down a giant redwood" (P, 61). Nonetheless, he believed that if the coalition of the American Right is to remain intact and achieve salutary ends, it has to protect the social groups within society from the encroachments of the national state—it has to be a conservative coalition.

SOCIOLOGY AND HISTORY

To treat Nisbet's reflections on sociology and history, the two fields in which he wrote and taught, might seem to require straying from what I have called Nisbet's "grand theme," but this is not the case. As we have seen, the concept of "society," used in reference to the groups and associations intermediate between the individual and the state, was central to the conservative reaction to the French Revolution, and, according to Nisbet, sociology was born of this concept. Although none of the great nineteenth- and twentieth-century sociologists— Tocqueville, Comte, Marx, Durkheim, Toennies, Simmel, and Weber—considered himself a conservative, each carried the intellectual legacies of the first conservative eruption. Accordingly, this chapter opens by surveying Nisbet's view of the relationship between conservatism and sociology; proceeds to a brief account of Nisbet's view of sociology as an art form; and concludes with a description of Nisbet's critical analysis of the "idea of progress" in the histories of civilization and social change.

Conservatism and Sociology

In one of his first published articles, Nisbet observes, "Historians of social thought have been prone, on the whole, to regard sociology as a logical and continuous outcome of the ideas which had commanded the intellectual scene during the seventeenth and eighteenth centuries" (1943, 157). Such a view, Nisbet asserts, is false. The watchwords of that age—"individual," "contract," "reason," "progress," "freedom"—indicate a conceptual framework very different from the one assumed by early sociologists. A concern for "social groups"—the distinctive subject matter of sociology—Nisbet says, arose in direct response to the French Revolution. Inspired by Rousseau, the revolutionaries sought to destroy every outpost of traditional, intermediate society. "Under the impact of the Revolution the Church as a separate social organization was demolished and its clergy declared officials of the state. The guilds were destroyed in the name of *liberté du travail....* Education was declared to be a function of the state alone," and many of the rights of family over property and children were abolished (1943,159). Most Enlightenment thinkers were indifferent if not hostile to intermediate institutions, but Auguste Comte and other early sociologists lamented the breakdown of these institution in the wake of the Revolution. "It was the hope of rebuilding society in the sense of intermediate society that led Comte to the formulation of his Positive System" (1943, 161).

According to Nisbet, the intellectual grounds from which sociology emerged were cleared by conservatives. To be sure, he says, nineteenth-century thought in general maintained a faith in progress and in the liberation of individuals, but, "Sociology...from the very beginning borrowed heavily from the insights into society that such men as Burke, Bonald and Hegel had supplied" (1952, 172). Although conservatism had little direct influence on the age, conservative concepts and terms such as "*social, tradition, custom, institution, folk, community, organism, tissue,* and *collective* achieved almost overnight a prestige and function they had not known since the heyday of realist vs. nominalist thought in the Middle Ages" (emphasis in original) (c, 77).

Nisbet believes that the intellectual changes marked by the shift in language from the eighteenth to the nineteenth centuries must be accounted for in moral terms. "Theoretical problems in the social sciences always have a significant relation to the moral aspirations of an age" (1952, 168). The breakup of the old order caused by the French Revolution and mass democracy, on the one hand, and by the industrial revolution, on the other, created concerns virtually unknown to the Age of Enlightenment—concerns over the problems of individualism, urbanization, social disorganization, secularism, bureaucratization, estrangement, and insecurity. These were and are largely moral concerns and, however "abstract the ideas may eventually become, however neutral they may come to seem to scientists and theorists, they do not ever really divest themselves of their moral origins" (st, 18). Certainly, these origins were more explicit in the writings of Burke, de Maistre, or Hegel than in those of Durkheim, Weber, and Simmel, but the concerns are the same; the roots of modern sociology, Nisbet says, run much more deeply in the conservative tradition than in liberal-radical systems of thought. This is not to suggest a strict genetic relationship between conservatism and sociology or that the sociologists merely restated conservative propositions. "The point is, the conservatives were instrumental in *identifying* the world of institutions and their growths—identifying this world for the uses of nineteenth-century scholarship and science—simply by virtue of their sustained *eulogy* of it at the expense of the hated, 'metaphysical' world of natural law and natural rights" (c, 76).

Nisbet probes the connection between conservatism and sociology in a number of his writings but explores this connection most fully in *The Sociological Tradition*, first published in 1966 (and republished by Transaction Press in 1993). This book is a major theoretical accomplishment in its own right, and it is arguably the best secondary account of classical sociological theory ever written in the English language. Its approach is also unique among books on sociological theory. Nisbet records that most texts in the history of thought take one or the other of two approaches: (1) by analyzing individual thinkers themselves or (2) by focusing not on an individual but on a system, school, or "ism." Both approaches can be fruitful, but each has problems. In the first, "ideas are treated as extensions or shadows of single individuals rather than as the distinguishable structures of meaning, perspective, and allegiance that major ideas so plainly are in the history of civilization." In the second, ideas are reified, taken as irreducible; and the systems "tend to become lifeless" (ST, 3-4). Consequently, Nisbet opts for a third approach, "one that begins with neither the man nor the system, but with the ideas which are elements of the system." He organizes his history of sociological thought by focusing on what he calls, following Arthur Lovejoy, "unit-ideas." In any field, such ideas, he says, must have generality, continuity, and distinction, and provide a perspective or framework. In applying these criteria, Nisbet discerns five essential unit-ideas of sociology, each of which preoccupied the classical sociological theorists and which together reveal the conservative origins of the field. The five are: *community, authority, status,* the *sacred,* and *alienation.*

Each of these ideas is linked to "a conceptual opposite, to a kind of antithesis, from which it derives much of its continuing meaning in the sociological tradition" (ST, 6). Nisbet takes 250 pages to describe these unit-ideas and their antitheses as developed by the classical sociologists, all of which cannot be discussed in these few pages. But that is not necessary. These ideas and their antitheses link up to what has already been described. *Community*, of course, refers not merely to local community but also to religion, work, family, and voluntary associations—to those social groups mediating between the individual and the state which were defended first by the conservatives and rediscovered by the likes of Tocqueville, Comte, Toennies, and Durkheim. The antithesis of community is *society*, not as the composite of communities, but rather as *Gesellschaft*, the large-scale, impersonal institutions at whose center contractual ties are to be found. *Authority* refers to the inner order of institutions such as church, family, or guild, legitimized by social function, tradition, or custom. Because it is so deeply embedded in social functions in traditional societies, "authority is hardly recognizable as having separate or even distinguishable identity" (ST, 107). The antithesis of authority, needless to say, is *power*. Whereas "the image of social authority is cast from materials drawn from the old regime; the image of political power—rational, centralized and popular—[is] from the legislative pattern of the Revolution" (ST, 112). "*Status* is the individual's position in the hierarchy of prestige and influence that characterizes every community or association" (ST, 6). Its conceptual opposite is *class*, which refers not to the hierarchies of traditional communities but to the new hierarchies created by the processes of individualization, leveling, and fragmentation associated with modern economic and political upheavals (ST, 177). *Sacred* refers "to the totality of myth, ritual, sacrament, dogma, and the mores in human behavior; to the whole area of individual motivation and social organization that transcends the utilitarian or rational and draws its vitality from what Weber called charisma and Simmel piety" (ST, 221). The opposite of sacred is the profane or *secular*, which refers to the merely utilitarian or rational. Finally, *alienation* refers to the estranged, anomic, and rootless sense one has when cut off from community and moral purpose. Alienation does not have an opposite; it is, rather, an inversion of *progress*. Alienation is caused by the very forces which some thinkers in the nineteenth century hailed as progress (see ST, 264-270).

These unit-ideas do not exhaust sociological concerns, according to Nisbet, but they are definitive of the field. Economists, political scientists, psychologists, and anthropologists seem to have no knowledge of any significant impact of these ideas. They do, though, preoccupy the likes of Durkheim, Simmel, and Weber; and from our vantage point, "it is possible to see deep currents of conservatism in the writing of all three men, currents running against the stream of overt political affiliation." For each of these men there is a "tension between the values of political liberalism and the values of a humanistic or cultural conservatism, however reluctant this conservatism might be" (ST, 17).

Tensions of this sort, Nisbet reminds us, have been central historically to "golden ages," and the period between 1830 and 1900 Nisbet calls "the golden age of sociology." "Its contextual frame was the conflict between two social orders: the feudal-traditional and the democratic-capitalist," and the sociological ideas that emerged in the period between Tocqueville and Weber still determine the way we see our social world today (ST, 316). Nonetheless, Nisbet continues, because the democratic and industrial revolutions have triumphed so completely, these tensions cannot today be felt vividly. "It thus becomes ever more difficult to squeeze creative juices out of the classic antitheses, that, for a hundred years, have provided theoretical structure for sociology.... It becomes ever more difficult to extract new essence, new hypothesis, new conclusion, from them. Distinctions become ever more tenuous, examples ever more repetitive, vital subject matter ever more elusive" (ST, 318).

If a new idea system does appear, Nisbet says in concluding *The Sociological Tradition*, "it will not be the consequence of methodology, much less of computers, of mass data gathering and retrieval, or of problem definition however rigorous, or research design however aseptic. It will be the consequence, rather, of intellectual processes which the scientist shares with the artist: ironic imagination, aggressive intuition, each given discipline by reason and root in reality" (ST, 319). Not one of the unit-ideas of classical sociology, Nisbet observes, came from logical-empirical analysis, at least not alone. "Without exception, each of these ideas is the result of thought processes—imagination, vision, intuition—that bear as much relation to the artist as to the scientist" (ST, 18-19).

Sociology as an Art Form

The words in the title of this section, which appear in *The Sociological Tradition*, are drawn directly from an article Nisbet wrote in 1962 entitled "Sociology as an Art Form." In 1976, Nisbet expanded this article into a small book, with the same title, published by Oxford University Press. The book is both descriptive and prescriptive. Nisbet writes that great sociological thinking is inspirited by the same creative impulses that lie behind great art, the recognition of which, he believes, should reorient sociology away from "scientism" toward more imaginative and illuminating endeavors. By "scientism," Nisbet means "science with the spirit of discovery and creation left out" (SAF, 4). Sociology, he believes, is plagued by scientism, the product of methodological obsessions, an absurd notion of "theory construction," and, most fundamentally, a failure to distinguish between the *logic of discovery* and the *logic of demonstration*. The latter is "properly subject to rules and prescriptions." It is given to codification and presentation in methodology and "theory construction" textbooks. The logic of discovery, on the other hand, cannot be codified, and no amount of effort to follow the rules of methodology and "theory construction" will ever add a whit of what is needed for genuine discovery, according to Nisbet (SAF, 5). Nisbet does not deny that sociology is one of the sciences, but he insists that it is also one of the arts, "nourished …by precisely the same kinds of creative imagination which are found in such areas as music, painting, poetry, the novel and drama." This kinship, though, is not limited to sociology. "Behind the creative act in any science, physical or social, lies a form and intensity of imagination, a utilization of intuition…that is not different in nature from what we have learned of the creative process in the arts" (SAF, 9). Science and art are distinguished by their respective modes of demonstration but not by their processes of discovery. Indeed, in the case of sociology the nature of these processes is strikingly similar to the arts in that both involve what Weber called *Verstehen*, a sympathetic or empathetic understanding that "penetrates to the realm of feeling, motivation and spirit" (SAF, 12). *Verstehen* is not a matter of method but of reverie, musing, and simple association of the individual's creative faculties.

Nisbet further claims that the themes or "unit-ideas" that occupied the attention of the classical sociologists during sociology's "golden age"—community, authority, status, the sacred, and alienation—are the themes of "Blake, Coleridge,

Balzac or Dickens among writers and of Hogarth, David, Millet or Daumier among those who made line, light and shadow serve the cause of illuminating reality" (SAF, 41). Just as in literature and painting the chief means for conveying these themes was through landscapes and portraits, so too, Nisbet says, sociologists created sociological landscapes and sociological portraits. Sociological landscapes show the changing social scenery created by the democratic and industrial revolutions—the masses, the concentration of state power, the factory system, and the urban metropolis. Sociological portraits are the ideal-typical or role-typical portraits found in the works of the golden age sociologists—the bourgeois, the worker, the bureaucrat and the intellectual (SAF, 42-92).

According to Nisbet, whether created by the artist or by the sociologist, landscapes and portraits present a problem: they are static, making it necessary to foster "the illusion of motion." The artist's problem, Nisbet records Etienne Gilson observing, "is to obtain from the solid and immobile objects produced by his art in expression of movement, of becoming, and, in short, life." Similarly, "Few things matter as much to the sociologists of the nineteenth century as, in Comte's phrasing, the uniting of statics and dynamics; that is, the achievement, through one systematic set of principles, of an explanation of structure or order on the one hand and of change and development on the other" (SAF, 94). The typical solution to this problem among the sociologists was to postulate, as immanent within the structure of society, a principle of progress, evolution, and inevitable change. "Development, in short, was omnipresent as an idea or theme in nineteenth-century thought" (SAF, 103). But, as noted above, for the nineteenth-century sociologists, alienation was as inevitable as progress, its inversion. "Throughout the nineteenth century, side by side with the spirit of progress that so plainly animates the minds of the larger number of philosophers and social scientists, there is to be seen slowly but certainly developing a kind of malaise affecting the very premises on which the spirit of progress rested" (SAF, 115). The nineteenth-century efforts to create the illusion of motion fostered both the "idea of progress" and an acknowledgment of what Nisbet calls "the rust of progress."

Developmentalism and the Idea of Progress

"During the period of 1750-1900," Nisbet says, "the idea of progress reached its zenith in the Western mind in popular as well as scholarly circles. From being *one* of the important ideas in the West it became the dominant idea..." (HIP, 171). Teleological typologies and stages were rife in historical accounts of institutions and social change. This is the age of rude versus polished (Ferguson), status versus contract (Maine), organismic versus individualistic (Gierke), homogeneous versus heterogeneous (Spencer), *Gemeinschaft* vs *Gesellschaft* (Toennies), me-

chanical vs organic (Durkheim), traditional vs rational-bureau-
cratic (Weber), and of stages such as theological, metaphysical,
positivistic (Comte), hunting, herding, agricultural, and commercial (Montesquieu and Smith), and primitive communism,
slavery, feudalism, capitalism, socialism (Marx). According to
each of these theoretical schemes, progress was immanent
within the structure of institutions, and other important ideas—
liberty, equality, justice, popular sovereignty—were treated
within the developmental context implied by the idea of
progress.

Nisbet investigates the idea of progress in numerous articles and in two books, *Social Change and History* (1969) and
History of the Idea of Progress (1980, republished by Transaction
Press in 1993). In each of these works Nisbet analyzes at length
the developmental theories of the late eighteenth and nineteenth
centuries. But this era is not his exclusive concern, because he
attempts to overcome two common misconceptions of the idea
of progress: first, that it is uniquely a modern idea and, second,
that it stems from secularism. Together these beliefs have led
analysts to associate the idea of progress solely with the eighteenth and nineteenth centuries. This era Nisbet calls the "heyday" of the idea of progress, but he argues that the origins of the
idea lie with Greek and Roman efforts to understand their past
and that the Christians continued and refined what the classical pagan philosophers began.

"Greek thought," Nisbet says, "was saturated with ideas of development and progress." Basic to Greek science was the concept of *physis*, translated by the Romans as *natura* or nature. "The *physis* of anything—dog, tree, kinship system, *polis*—was simply the pattern of growth and change that was held to be inherent in it, natural to its very structure or being" (MMS, 39-40). The task of Greek science was to identify the *physis* of whatever object of study. Thus, for example, regarding the *physis* of the social/political order, both Plato and Aristotle imagined development and progress that occurred, in Plato's words, "step by step" over "many generations."[1] And Plato and Aristotle were far from alone among the Greeks. Hesiod, Aeschylus, Sophocles, Protagoras, and Thucydides each wrote of human development over the ages (SCH, 15-61 and HIP, 13-26). Similarly, Nisbet continues, among the Romans, progress was a prominent theme in several of Seneca's discourses, but it was Lucretius who first used the term "progress"—indeed "step by step progression," *pedetemtim progredientes*—and who is the philosopher of progress *non pareil* among Latin philosophers (HIP, 37-46).

"Christianity," Nisbet says, "united the Greek belief in natural growth through time with the Jewish conception of sacred history, that is, history that could not have been other than it actually was" (P, 239). From this unity arose the Christian, especially Augustinian, belief in historical necessity and the ecumenical ideal of the unity of all mankind (see HIP, 59-76). "All of the essential ideas involved in the philosophy of progress—slow, gradual and continuous advance through time of all mankind, in a pattern of successively higher stages of development, the whole process revealing necessity, direction and purpose—are to be found in the Christian philosophy of history" (P, 239). From Augustinian through medieval currents, down to the Puritans, who combined the idea of advancing knowledge with the idea of advancing morality, the Christian idea of progress has been among the most powerful ideas in Western history. Indeed, as Nisbet argues, "the move from the Christian to the 'modern' conception of progress was short and uncomplicated" (P, 240). God's Providence was merely replaced by "natural causes." Yet even this replacement occurred step by step. In the thinking of Enlightenment figures such as Turgot, Lessing, and Kant, human ascent was deemed inevitable by reason of Providential *and* natural causes. For many Enlightenment figures, God and nature were not sworn enemies.

Nonetheless, Providence was all but completely eclipsed by natural causes in the nineteenth century when the idea of progress became a popular faith "on the scale of a religion." According to the major social evolutionary theorists of the age, change was natural, directional, immanent, continuous, necessary, and issued from uniform causes (SCH, 166-188). It was an age in which the modern West was deemed, by the comparative method, to be the human pinnacle against which other civilizations, and earlier

Western epochs, could be measured. To be sure, progress' inversion—alienation—was also described by nineteenth-century philosophers and sociologists, but this was considered the inevitable "rust" of progress. Though unfortunate, it was deemed to be greatly outweighed by the benefits of progress.

Given Nisbet's conservative disposition, he naturally doubts the root assumptions of social evolutionary or developmental theories. "Change is," he says, "*not* natural, *not* normal, much less ubiquitous and constant. Fixity is.... If we look at actual social behavior, in place and in time, we find over and over that persistence in time is the far more common condition of things" (SCH, 270). Change is also not directional. "Patterns, rhythms, trends are inescapably subjective. There is no inherent relation to the data. However persuasive a given 'direction' may be to our acquired interests or values, it has no independent or objective validity" (SCH, 285). Consequently, the record is littered with false predictions by social theorists misdirected by directional conceptions of history and social change. Marx is merely the most spectacular example in this regard. Similarly, change is not immanent and continuous. "Overwhelmingly, major change is the consequence of impact from outside the entity or system of behavior that is the subject of our attention" (MMS, 65). Change is, therefore, contingent and episodic. And, finally, change is not uniform. There are, Nisbet says, constants in human nature, but "constants," he observes, "are ordinarily of little help in accounting for variables." Thus, "Greed, lust, ambition, covetousness, like love, altruism, charity, and compassion have always been with us in one degree or other," but what is constant cannot be invoked to explain what is changeable (SCH, 298).

What might surprise is that although Nisbet questions the idea of progress as a description of history and social change, he still laments its current moribund state because it has been "a powerful intellectual force behind Western civilization's spectacular achievements" and the cement linking persons to the past and, more important, to the future. Nisbet anticipated Richard Gill's recent argument that devotion to posterity requires belief in the idea of progress.[2] The current condition of the idea of progress Nisbet accounts for chiefly in terms of our religious circumstances. "The idea was…born of religion in the classical world, sustained by religion from the third century on, and now threatens to die from the loss of religious sustenance. For no century in Western history has proved to be as nonreligious, irreligious, and antireligious in its major currents of philosophy, art, literature and science as is the twentieth" (P, 241-242).

As to what the future might bring, Nisbet concludes *History of the Idea of Progress* on a note of optimism. He says that if we take stock of the lessons of the past, our circumstance is not likely to persist. We cannot be certain, but, he says, "we can take some reasonable guidance, I believe, first from the fact that never in history have periods of culture such as our own lasted for very long. They are destroyed by all the forces which constitute their essence. How can any society or age last very long if it lacks or is steadily losing the minimal requirements for a society—such requirements being the very opposite of the egoistic and hedonistic elements that dominate Western culture today?" He takes as a second reason for believing that change is imminent "the faint, possibly illusory, signs of the beginnings of a religious renewal in Western Civilization, notably in America" (HIP, 356). He continues by observing that there are some signs of a declining faith in politics and that if this apparent decline is "real and lasting, the case is all the stronger for a recrudescence of religion" (HIP, 356). In any event, it is only "in the context of a true culture," Nisbet argues, "in which the core is a deep and wide sense of the *sacred*" that we are "likely to regain the vital conditions of progress itself and of faith in progress—past, present and future" (HIP, 357). Progress is not a matter of historical law and inevitability. Yet true progress, without alienation, Nisbet believed, is possible if we acknowledge the sacred, submit our hedonistic egoism to the authority of community, and shed our faith in politics as a means to salvation.

STATISM OR A NEW LAISSEZ-FAIRE?

IN *History of the Idea of Progress,* Nisbet is both optimistic and pessimistic—optimistic concerning the prospects of Western civilization, but pessimistic when assessing the social sciences. He states that "the contributions of the social sciences have been minimal when not actually counterproductive, and that in so many of the projects of social reconstruction designed by social scientists for government execution more harm than good has been the result—as in benignly intended but disastrous 'wars' against poverty, ethnic discrimination, poor housing, slums and crime" (HIP, 347). So extensive have the latter efforts been that elsewhere Nisbet says, "Today, given the extent to which all the social sciences have become monopolized by political values and aspirations, it would be more correct if they were called political sciences" (P, 287).

Nisbet does not exaggerate much here. Typically, contemporary social scientists view the pluralistic social world as a contemptible source of inequality, parochial fears of cosmopolitan rationality, and continuing prejudice. Just as typically, they are economic determinists who believe that the solutions to the problems of the social world lie with the state. Among sociologists in particular, political monism, knowingly or unknowingly inspired by Rousseau, is the reigning perspective on the social order.

This final chapter appraises Nisbet's work and legacy. Chiefly, it analyzes a contemporary example of political monism to show that the weight of *empirical evidence* sustains Nisbet's social pluralistic perspective, and not political monism. The example of the monistic perspective is the "updated edition" of *Habits of the Heart*, written by Robert Bellah and four junior coauthors—for two reasons. First, it is one of the most widely read books written by sociologists in the last several decades; and, second, it is known as one of a handful of very influential "communitarian" works. Thus, it in some measure represents both sociology and an influential brand of "communitarianism." It is also, alas, sociologically very dubious in respect to empirical evidence, and its form of "communitarianism," focused on "national community," is reflexively antipathetic to "community" in any meaningful sense of the term. The facts seem to confirm Nisbet's beliefs that American social problems result chiefly from the breakdown of intermediate institutions, especially the family, and that this requires a new laissez-faire toward the social group or association.

Before pursing this analysis, however, brief commentary on another, secondary, aim: expanding Nisbet's conception of social pluralism to include the classical liberalism of John Locke; the Baron de Montesquieu; and the Scottish moralists, especially David Hume, Adam Ferguson, and Adam Smith. Although Nisbet refers to each of these thinkers in his writing, he treats none of them as representative of social pluralism.[1] This, I believe, is unfortunate. For we are naturally social or communal, according to the classical liberals; and, among other things, the social pluralism advocated by the classical liberals led directly, via Tocqueville's reading of Montesquieu (the first to write of "secondary" and "intermediate" groups), to Tocquevillian pluralism and, via Madison's reading of Montesquieu and Hume, to the social pluralism of the American Constitution. In fact, a very strong case can be made for Montesquieu and the Scottish moralists as the first social scientists. In any event, before taking on Bellah and contemporary political monism, it should be clear that classical liberalism is a rich resource of social pluralistic thinking and has been tremendously important historically.

But more than simply demonstrating the fundamental compatibility of Nisbet's worldview and classical liberalism, I hope to begin to reconcile two often antagonistic branches of contemporary social pluralism. If contemporary traditionalists and those who today invoke the classical liberal tradition were true to their avowed roots, little would separate them and they could more successfully combat political monism.

Classical Liberalism and Social Pluralism

In *The Quest for Community*, Nisbet states, "When the basic principles of modern liberalism were being formulated by such men as Locke, Montesquieu, Adam Smith and Jefferson, the image of man luminous in the philosophical mind was an image constructed out of such traits as sovereign reason, stability, security and indestructible motivations toward freedom and order. Man, abstract man, was deemed to be inherently self-sufficing, equipped by nature with both the instincts and the reason that could make him autonomous" (QC, 225). "The philosophy of individualism," he continues, "became a rationalist psychology devoted to the ends of the release of man from the old and a sociology based upon the view that groups and institutions are at best mere reflections of the solid and ineffaceable fact of the individual" (QC, 226; also see TA, 277, and P, 210-217). Specifically regarding Locke, he says that although Locke "could give more explicit emphasis to individual rights, the fact remains that it was Hobbes's own brilliant sketching of the political environment of individualism that made the later system possible. In many senses Locke is a derivative thinker. Hobbes was his master in all important respects" (QC, 138; SP, 33).

Such views are common enough, but they are misleading. The classical liberals believe, as does Nisbet, that human beings are by nature sociable and communal. According to them, humans subsisted before the emergence of the state in conjugal bands held together by natural affection and obligation. Thus their meager property, gained by labor, was communal, but while community members were devoted to each other, they were distrustful and hateful of strangers. The original condition was not one of a war of all against all, as Hobbes imagined. It was a war of some against some—a far more bloody war because it was fired by communal devotion. By contrast, political society, the classical liberals hold, is not natural but rather the human solution to the problems of innate partiality and conflict over accumulated property. But in both—political societies and natural, primitive societies—communal affection and obligation are *naturally* limited.

Given the extent of nation-states, the classical liberals distinguished between two realms: a communal, private realm; and a public, primarily commercial, realm.[2] These two realms are arranged on very different principles, according to the classical liberals. Whereas the private realm relies upon concern for some intimate few, the public realm relies upon a self-interest that is indiscriminate and indifferent to the qualities of strangers. Whereas the private realm depends upon the original and natural sentiments of benevolence, the public realm depends upon passionless, universal justice sustained by utilitarian reason. Whereas our status in the private realm is largely ascribed and our relationships are beyond mere contracts and codified laws, in the public realm our relationships are contractual and governed by laws. And whereas the private or communal realm is sustained by the accretion of discrete and exceptional benevolent acts, universal justice sustains public relations systemically; exceptional or particularistic treatment is regarded as vicious because it destroys impartial justice.

But this substantial treatment of the private realm by the classical liberals is regularly neglected by critics. Such neglect, I suspect, accounts for Nisbet's portrayal of Locke as an Hobbesian clone. Yet, a brief inspection of *The Second Treatise* shows that Locke treats two institutions in equal measure, the family and government: the family is a natural institution, and parents have a natural, noncontractual and unilateral obligation to raise their children to maturity. For the classical liberals, the private realm is at least as important as the public realm, and misconceptions of classical liberalism necessarily follow from a failure to distinguish between their view of the private and public realms—which, I believe, Nisbet demonstrates.

Properly understood, the ideals of the classical liberals in their views of civil society—especially those of Montesquieu and the Scottish moralists—converge with Nisbet's. Montesquieu and the Scottish moralists describe the history of civil society as a transition from small homogeneous societies to large pluralistic nations. Human nature was everywhere, but our passions and interests are channeled differently by changed institutions in different circumstances. Small societies—tribal societies or city-states—depend upon the submission of the individual to the good of the whole. They are sustained by the similarity of conscience or consciousness and the pursuit of common aims.

Sparta was the "prodigy" among ancient regimes (to use Hume's term) for Montesquieu and the Scottish moralists.[3] Although opposed to the common bent of human nature, the Spartan regime was suited to its social conditions because of its patriotic virtue, anticommercial code, poverty, communal tables, and, of course, its intense ferocity. Nonetheless, the sort of consensus and solidarity represented by Sparta (admired by Rousseau, criticized by Nisbet, and, as we will see, recommended by Bellah and his co-authors) is neither possible nor desirable in large nation-states, according to the classical liberals. As Hume says, attempts to organize nation-states on the principles of perfect virtue and "the community of goods" lead to the "total dissolution of society."[4] Ironically, while individual and social or factional differences cause disorder within small societies, properly arranged, such differences encourage peace and order within large nations. Therefore, rather than attempting to eliminate the social differences, they are to be encouraged so that no single group can dominate the others. Politically, this means the partitioning of power.[5] Culturally, this means social pluralism, the presence of "secondary" or "intermediate" groups, and institutionalized tolerance.[6] And economically, this means that economies should be arranged so that social differences—be they ethnic, religious, or other—are insignificant in the marketplace.[7]

For these authors, as for Nisbet, the modern state should possess universal criminal, civil, and commercial laws, and laws permitting freedom of association. Such a state fosters spontaneous sociability and the formation of those social groups needed for civil and civic improvement. But for these thinkers, as for Nisbet, however, modern civil society also has a private side, a familiar realm allowing for and requiring the submission of individual desires to the needs of particular others. Within this realm, virtue is formed; we are regulated by the approbation and disapprobation of our loved ones; and we undertake positive acts aimed at common ends—genuine corporate acts. According to the classical liberal scheme, just as there are benevolent and self-interested sides to our nature, so there are two broad institutional contexts within modern civil society.

Still, as important as this distinction is, because the natural needs pursued within the public context of civil society are provided by the intimate, primarily conjugal, realm. For Smith, therefore, it may not simply be "from the benevolence of the butcher, the brewer or the baker that we expect our dinner, but from their regard to their own interest," and, as motives for their labor, from benevolence toward those who sit at their respective tables.[8] Montesquieu and Smith, moreover, anticipate Nisbet's view of the social role of private religion. Both favored the disestablishment of state religion, freedom of religious conscience, and religious pluralism; and both recognized long before Max Weber the role played by certain forms of religion in the advancement of civil liberty and in the fostering of work motives essential to the commercial order. Smith, for example, distinguishes between established religions and sects, seeing the former as characterized by a "loose set" of morals congenial to the dissipated ways of the aristocracy, and the latter favored by "common people," as promoting an orderly and austere system of morals that, when moderated by education, sponsors economic security and advancement.[9]

An even deeper continuity between the private and public sides of civil society is revealed by the Scottish moralists in their social or moral psychology. For within the flowing narrative of individual lives, they maintain, experiences within these two realms are continuous, and any social experience at all is possible only because of the psychological capacity all humans possess for imaginatively transporting themselves into the situation of others. This capacity Smith, following Hume, calls "sympathy."[10] Sympathy, he says, is what enables us to assess the propriety and merit of others' acts. We approve benevolent and just acts, just as we disapprove ungracious and unjust acts, accord-

ing to our sympathies. Additionally, Smith believed, the degree
to which we can overcome our selfish inclinations and make
accurate judgments of ourselves is achieved according to the
previous experiences we have had in judging the acts of others.
These experiences lead us to take the attitude of, to use Smith's
words, a "man in general," "an impartial spectator," when assessing ourselves. "I, divide myself, as it were, into two persons;
and that I, the examiner and judge, represents a different character from the other I, the person whose conduct is examined
into and judged of."[11] Others serve as our looking glass when
we appraise ourselves. Although Nisbet fails to acknowledge
that the Scottish moralists first described this process (he attributes the description to twentieth-century American sources),
he says this process is "at the bottom of culture" and "is the very
stuff of human personality, character, self and identity" (SB, 59).[12]

Human "approbativeness," to use Arthur Lovejoy's term—
both self-approbation/disapprobation and the approbation/dis-
approbation of others—is of huge importance to the eighteenth-
century theorists hoping to maintain the independence of civil
society from state power.[13] These theorists believed we are
nudged toward goodness, genuine "praiseworthiness," when we
seek honor and praise and when we hope to avoid the blame
and censure of our significant fellows. Indeed, for the classical
liberals as much as for Nisbet, these checks upon temptations
to evil are conceived as replacing the Hobbesian check. Civil

society is deemed capable of moral self-regulation, where such regulation is seen as local and for the most part informal. We can try to probe the motives of people at a distance, but morally responsible and effective responses require sustained contact and close inspection. Thus, for Smith, physical and social proximity determine the natural limits of our actions towards others, and those closest to us—our *families, friends,* and *neighbors*—are recommended to our care.[14] Universal loyalty and universal community are simply impossible, according to Smith. He speaks of "universal benevolence," a vague sense supportive of justice; yet, he says, it is the source of "no solid happiness" and that the "administration of the great system of the universe...the core of the happiness of all rational and sensible beings, is the business of God and not of man."[15] Our duties lie close to home: genuine benevolence looks its object in the eye.

Regarding their political influence, it would be difficult to overestimate the importance of Locke, Montesquieu, and the Scottish moralists within America, and their influence upon America's founding generation contributed to the subdued and constrained tendencies of the American Revolution described by Nisbet (MMS, 167-185). More fundamentally, Locke and especially Montesquieu and the Scottish moralists are important for their purer sociological observations and concepts that lie at the source of their political views. Among their concepts that have wide currency among contemporary sociologists are the division of labor and the labor theory of value; the principle of unintended consequences; the distinction between social solidarity that depends upon resemblances and social solidarity that depends upon differences; the concept of the looking-glass self; the concept of the generalized other or the impartial spectator; the phases of the I, or the "I and Me"; the idea of sympathy or empathy as the psychological capacity essential to human group life; and the idea that the Protestant sects were essential to the development of capitalism. In addition, the ideas of the Scottish moralists clearly inspired the concepts of "primary groups," "consciousness of kind," and "ethnocentrism"—ideas among the most prominent in early American sociology.[16]

Mentioning the profound importance of these classical liberals in forming modern sociological thinking in no way diminishes Nisbet's claims concerning the influence of conservatism upon social concepts and thinking. I merely wish to point out the extraordinary compatibility of what Nisbet discusses as conservatism and what is known as "classical liberalism." Specifically, the similarities are remarkable between Smith's view of "universal benevolence" and Burke's views of the same, as demonstrated in his broadside against Rousseau. Smith discussed "universal benevolence" in the 1790 edition of the *Theory of Moral Sentiments* and Burke used the term in his 1791 "Letter to a Member of the National Assembly." Smith's discussion of this concept follows immediately his criticisms of "men of system," which were clearly directed at the French revolutionaries. The two men shared much more than a common animus, however. As Nisbet acknowledges (C, 37), Burke reviewed the original 1759 edition of the *Theory*, calling it "one of the most beautiful fabrics of moral theory, that has perhaps ever appeared," and also *The Wealth of Nations*, describing it as "probably the most important book ever written."[17] Indeed, after Smith met Burke face-to-face, he said that Burke was the "only man I ever knew who thinks on economic subjects exactly as I do, without any previous communication having passed between us."[18] Burke was also a close acquaintance of Hume, who in fact mailed a copy of Smith's *Theory of Moral Sentiments* to Burke for review, and Burke revered Montesquieu above all other modern moralists. Montesquieu, he said, was "a genius not born in every country or every time; a man gifted by nature with a penetrating aquiline eye; with a judgement prepared with the most extensive erudition; with a herculean robustness of mind, and nerves not to be broken with labor; a man who could spend twenty years in one pursuit" (researching *The Spirit of the Laws*).[19] Burke continues for another twenty-five lines, ratcheting his compliments upward as he goes.

Nisbet, I believe, is correct to prefer the language of pluralism versus monism in his accounts of modern social and political philosophies. Certainly, it makes no sense to refer to Burke as a "conservative" if Smith or any of the other classical liberals is taken a "liberal." The language of "pluralism" and "monism" captures the central difference among modern thinkers, whatever their superficial differences; and by this conceptual scheme, so nicely outlined by Nisbet, both the classical liberals and traditionalists, such as Burke and Nisbet himself, are among the most important social pluralists.

Monistic and Pluralistic Communitarianism

Whether speaking of the institutions of civil society, as described by classical liberals, or of "communities," as conceived by Nisbet, the evidence is strong that the well-being of society depends upon the health and vibrancy of intermediate institutions. Certainly, massive evidence is provided by the Soviet experience. For decades those under the Marxian spell denounced the intermediate communities of civil society as sources of human degradation, illegitimate hierarchy, and social tyranny, the perceived solution to which was a redemptive political community. But harsh experience proved that the political tyranny inherent in this solution to the supposed problems of civil society was enervating at its most benign and brutal at its worst. Indeed, as Nisbet seemed to know beforehand (see PA, *passim*), after the Soviet empire disintegrated, the recovery of its former subjugated nations depended almost entirely upon the degree to which their intermediate institutions had been eliminated; those nations whose social infrastructure had remained largely in place attained a quick measure of order and prosperity, while those nations whose intermediate institutions were overwhelmed have so far failed to reestablish social order and prosperity—and may never do so.

Such evidence has not dampened the enthusiasm of political monists such as Robert Bellah, however, and these pages will focus on the American context by analyzing several claims made in the new introduction to *Habits of the Heart*. I do this in order to convey a current and influential example of what Nisbet calls political monism, and in order to make as concrete a case as possible for Nisbet's pluralistic communitarianism. The facts, I believe, are all on Nisbet's side. The main sources of "cancerous individualism" (as Bellah calls it), and other American problems, are the failings of the institutions within the "inner circle" of communities, *especially within the family*, just as Nisbet argues and Bellah denies.[20] Nisbet asserts, in fact, that the egalitarian ethos is now causing as much damage "to the smaller, more intimate and subjective areas of family, marriage, and other personal relations" as it is to public institutions (PA, 117). Bellah, on the other hand, admires egalitarian personal relations and believes they are to be admired, while economic inequality must be ameliorated. A quintessential political monist, Bellah sees most social problems as caused by economic conditions, the solutions to which are statist solutions.

The new introduction to *Habits of the Heart* is somewhat

novel among Bellah's many writings because it is filled with so many (easily manipulated) empirical claims. Its worldview, however, has been at the center of Bellah's written work since at least the mid-1960s. Its main features are Rousseauian: a belief in political participation as an end in itself; a deep fear of egoism and economic inequality; the need to submit the natural inclinations of individuals to a socially constructed "common good"; the conviction that American social problems result exclusively from the misarrangement of "the large structures of the economy and state," not from the deficiencies of "face-to-face" communities; and a fervent belief in the unifying, equalizing, and redemptive powers of the state. Bellah's worldview contrasts with Nisbet's point for point and is what Nisbet would describe as "a blend of rigorous social nihilism and political affirmation" (SP, 8).

The new introduction to *Habits of the Heart* emphasizes several American trends, including the globalization of the economy, the stagnating wages of the majority of men, the widening gap between the "haves" and the "have nots," the middle class exit from the cities, and the geographic and institutional secession of the richest Americans. In accord with Robert Reich and Michael Lind, the authors speak of three American social classes: the "underclass," the poorest 10 percent of Americans; the "anxious class," the majority of Americans "trapped in the frenzy of effort it takes to preserve their standing"; and the "overclass," America's wealthiest fifth.[21] This distinction may be used here, but recall Nisbet's: although social class analysis is extremely common among "social scientists," social class "is of all affiliations the weakest in capitalist-democratic society" (PA, 121). Social class today is a mere aggregate. "Members" of social classes have no ties, and social classes share nothing with communities properly understood (SB, 197-221; ST, 174-220).

Taking the underclass first, herewith an egregious but representative sentence written by Bellah and his co-authors. "It is worth noting that five of six poor people in America are white and that poverty breeds drugs, violence and unstable families without regard to race."[22] The first of these two propositions is perplexing and obviously false. According to the Census Bureau, 14 percent of Americans live in poverty and, of these, 47 percent are white, not 83 percent as Bellah reports. The sentence's second proposition is far more significant because of all the ideological baggage it carries. According to this proposition, poverty breeds drugs, violence, and unstable families. Such a materialistic and mechanistic view is common enough among political monists. But there is little evidence to sustain this view. To maintain this view requires rapid blinking when comparing contemporary America with America in 1960. In 1960, 22 percent of Americans (55 percent of black Americans) lived in poverty.[23] Yet the percentage of all American out-of-wedlock births in 1960 was one-sixth its current percentage (where the increase in this percentage is a product of the decline in marital fertility and an increase in nonmarital fertility)[24]; the divorce rate was less than half its current rate; the rate of violent crime was between a half and a third what it is today[25];and, of course, drug-use was highly localized and comparatively rare. True, the divorce rate peaked in the early 1980s, and the violent crime and out-of-wedlock birth rates have recently declined. Still, none of these rates is at all close to the 1960 level. Recent unemployment rates and the poverty rate are significantly lower compared with the 1960 rates.

Because of discrimination, "structural" causes of poverty clearly existed in 1960. Just as clearly, however, the United States is far more meritocratic today than it was in 1960. Black women, for example, have achieved income parity with white women; the income of black males is on par with that of white men when adjusted for age, experience, and education; and black intact households are approaching income parity with comparable white households. Within this more meritocratic context, *the evidence does not indicate that poverty or any other structural factor produces unstable families. Rather, as Nisbet argues, it is unstable, i.e., fatherless, families that produce poverty, in addition to drug use and violence* (see PA, 118-122). Nisbet observes, "Single-parent families abound and grow in number by the day, a condition which virtually all studies unite in deploring—for psychological as well as social and economic reasons" (PA, 119). Families headed by females are five to six times as likely as male-headed families to be poor, and although poor children are more likely to be poor adults than other children, this is chiefly a result of fatherlessness.[26] Similarly, children in fatherless households are at least twice as likely as two-parent children to use drugs.[27] And the relationship between fatherlessness and crime is so strong that, if the effect of fatherlessness is eliminated, the relationship between poverty and crime and between race and crime disappears.[28] Seventy percent of all juveniles in state reform institutions, 70 percent of long-term prison inmates, 60 percent of rapists, and 72 percent of adolescent murderers are from fatherless homes.[29] Obviously, then, poverty as such does not cause crime. Nisbet records Eric Hoffer as observing, "If poverty were indeed the fundamental cause of crime, history would be about almost nothing else, for the vast majority of the people in world history have lived in poverty" (TA, 63).

Regarding violent crime, given media misrepresentations of the issue, it is worth noting that the decline in marriage is the root cause of increased violence against women. Generally, unmarried and divorced women are four times as likely as married woment to be victims of violent crime.[30] Regarding domestic violence specifically, the National Crime Victimization Survey reveals that unmarried women are four times more likely to suffer domestic abuse than married women and that divorced women are ten times more likely to be abuse victims than married women. *Marriage is the most important institutional hedge against violence aimed at women.* Similarly, the safest haven for children is one where they live with both biological parents. The vast majority of cases of neglect involve single mothers, and most of the cases of intimate sexual abuse involve live-in boy-friends or step-fathers. Indeed, one Canadian study of preschool children found that children in step-families are forty times more likely to suffer physical and sexual abuse than children living with both biological parents.[31]

In contrast with Nisbet, who eschews economic determin-ism (QC, 73-74, 98-106; 1962, xvii), Bellah and his co-authors refer to the work of William Julius Wilson and others who argue that the increases in crime, out-of-wedlock births, welfare de-pendency, and the like result from changes in the American economy.[32] According to this argument, since the mid-1960s, jobs, especially manufacturing jobs, have gone overseas or to the suburbs, and the middle class has followed the jobs to the suburbs. Urban males, according to the theory, have been espe-cially hard hit by these changes; because jobs are unavailable, idle and dispirited males forgo marriage, women bear children outside of marriage, welfare and poverty increase, and crime rises.[33] There is some truth to this argument, but the evidence suggests that economic conditions have only a small effect upon family composition and social pathologies. Indeed, numerous facts cannot be explained by Wilson's theory. For example, the population losses of American cities *preceded* the job losses, probably because of the dramatic increases in crime during the prosperous 1960s; and these losses accelerated in the 1970s in those cities under mandatory busing orders.[34] In the 1960s, the poverty rate fell by half, yet the number of people on welfare more than doubled.[35] The rise and fall of unemployment only modestly affects welfare rolls.[36] The social pathology in cities such as Atlanta and Washington, D.C., which have never been manufacturing centers, rivals or exceeds the pathology of traditional manufacturing cities like St. Louis and Chicago. And most significant, the marriage rates for employed males and highly educated males have plummeted. Regarding blacks specifically, for example, the decline in marriage among highly educated, employed black males differs very little from the decline among all black men.[37] Nisbet's doubts concerning materialistic theories are well grounded.

The problems of the inner city, Nisbet says, are largely the result of the federal government acting in ways that have destroyed localism. He suggests, for example, that " the greater part of the opposition to...busing springs directly from pride in and sense of attachment to neighborhood" (TA, 261). Similarly, he says, "the Federal bulldozer" has registered "destruction in the larger cities of old and tightly constituted communities," all in the name of "urban renewal" (TA, 261). According to Bellah et al., by contrast, the urban underclass suffers because the "predatory" overclass has abandoned its civic obligations. "Educated in the highly competitive atmosphere of excellent universities and graduate schools," the overclass has withdrawn to its gated communities becoming tight-fisted, tax-hating oligarchs.[38] Similarly, the anxious class—both black and white—has fled the cities as well. "Those left behind," we are told, "were then subjected to the systemic withdrawal of institutional support, both private and public.... Cities under increasing fiscal pressures closed schools, libraries, and clinics, and even police and fire stations in ghetto areas. Moreover, the most vulnerable left behind have to fend for themselves in a Hobbesian world...."[39] "The money that would have been required to provide an infrastructure of education and economic opportunity for those in chronic poverty was never spent."[40]

The images here of a "predatory" overclass and a "vulnerable" underclass speak volumes about the nature and extent of Bellah's stark ideology—an ideology devoid of subtlety or complexity. Rather than focusing upon this, though, consider something concrete within these images and close to the heart of Bellah's monistic worldview: namely, that material resources determine the quality of educational opportunities. This Nisbet denies (TA, 152-157) for reasons we will see momentarily, and the facts are clearly on his side. Neither international, national, or local data confirm a causal relationship between material resources and educational achievement. On a per student basis, the United States outspends virtually every other advanced industrialized nation and, in constant dollars, spends almost three times as much today as in 1960.[41] Yet our students are often at the bottom of the barrel on achievement tests administered internationally, and their average SAT scores are lower today than in 1960 even when adjusted for selectivity bias. On a per student basis, every state in the Union outspends the Japanese, yet the Japanese outperform American students dramatically on international tests of achievement.

Similarly, there is no systematic relationship between money spent and educational achievement among the fifty states and the District of Columbia.[42] National data reveal that several states—North Dakota, South Dakota, Idaho, and Utah—rank among the lowest in per pupil expenditures, but among the very highest on standardized test performance. Meanwhile, Minnesota ranks fairly high on each indicator; Mississippi ranks low on each; and Washington, D.C., outspends every state on a per pupil basis, yet it outperforms only South Carolina on standardized tests. Correlation does not sufficiently prove causation, but it is necessary; and on a national level, no correlation exists between material resources and student achievement. And to take one example of more localized data, among the eight Atlanta area school districts, per pupil expenditures have a negative association (-.70) with standardized test scores and a positive relationship (.90) with student attrition.[43] Indeed, since the Coleman Report in the mid-1960s, not one of the more than two hundred recent studies of the topic has found that material resources affect educational outcomes. These studies have not diminished the enthusiasm for leveling, but as Burke and Nisbet assert, "Those who attempt to level, never equalize" (C, 51).

Nisbet's perspective is far more instructive on educational matters than the materialistic view. He says, "We have discovered that the school, for all the vast sums of money spent on it, is not, by itself, particularly effective...the effectiveness of the school is greatest when it is united in a pupil's life with family" (TA, 259). He goes on to observe that the middle-class family has an "extraordinary effect upon motivations—economic, political, social, [and] educational.... Almost all of what we are prone to call middle-class ways of behavior are in fact middle-class *family* ways of behavior" (PA, 118). And: "A steady succession of studies has made clear the vital place the family holds in individual motivation toward education, reason and achievement" (TA, 253). Indeed, just as Nisbet argues, motivational and family variables account for most of the variation in educational achievement (TA, 80-84). What psychologists call "self-efficacy"—the belief that what happens to someone is a result of his actions, not that of external forces—is what most strongly correlates with educational success, and high self-efficacy is strongly associated with the stability of an intact household. In fact, the variable that best predicts educational achievement among the fifty states and the District of Columbia is the percentage of children in these different locations who live in two-parent households. Every study has found that children from intact households are at least twice as likely to be educational high achievers as single-parent children, and that single-parent children are more than twice as likely to give up on school altogether.[44]

To their credit, when countering the claims of those such as Charles Murray, who maintain that the material inducements of welfare account for increases in out-of-wedlock births and welfare dependency, Bellah and his co-authors recognize the problems of certain types of economistic explanations. They observe, "The facts that welfare payments, including Aid to Families with Dependent Children, have systematically declined in real dollars over the last twenty years and that they have fallen by half during the 1980s alone are ignored by those who tell this story...." Still, the tenacity of the authors' intellectual posture is revealed in the remainder of this sentence: "as is the fact that over 70 percent of those on welfare stay on it for less than two years, and over 90 percent for less than eight years."[45] This is true but by itself terribly misleading. In a statement cited by Bellah et al., William Julius Wilson correctly observes "that although most people who became poor during some point in their lives experience poverty for only one or two years, a substantial sub-population remains in poverty for a very long time. Indeed, these long-term poor constitute about 60 percent of those in poverty at any given point in time and are in a poverty spell that will last eight or more years."[46] But these two groups—the temporarily poor and persistently poor—are quite different in ways Bellah et al. fail to acknowledge. For as Andrew Cherlin records, most temporarily poor families have an adult male in the household, but the large majority of the persistently poor are headed by females. According to one report, a child born out of wedlock today is thirty times more likely to live in persistent poverty than a child from an intact household. Indeed, according to three Census Bureau researchers, the increase in the number of female-headed households has been the *chief* cause of the widening gap in household incomes.[47]

The underclass, according to Bellah and his co-authors, assuages the scruples of the overclass and the anxious middle class. They assert that "the underclass story, which involves blaming the victims rather than recognizing the catastrophic economic and political failure of American society, serves to sooth the conscience of the affluent, and it even allows them to wax indignant at the cost of welfare in a time of expanding deficits."[48] Similarly, "the shrinking middle class, shorn of its postwar job security by the pressure of global competitiveness, is tempted to look down at those worse off as the source of our national problems."[49]

In any event, middle-class anxiety and fears, we are told, are great. This too Nisbet believed. But, whereas Nisbet attributed middle-class anxiety and fears to a lack of clear purpose, status, continuity, and community membership (QC, 73), Bellah et al. say that the middle or "anxious" class fears "downsizing, re-engineered jobs and the pink slip of dismissal." The middle class has a "gnawing uncertainty" about the future of its jobs and adequate income.[50] And all of this is justified, according to Bellah et al., in that Americans have "significantly higher rates of economic deprivation" than citizens of the industrial nations of East Asia and Europe.[51]

Bellah's analysis is, frankly, more a mixture of nostalgia, fantasy, and hyperbole than social science. Over the last twenty years the American economy has been the envy of the world because of its capacity for generating jobs while avoiding inflation. The false images created by Bellah and his co-authors mirror those of the American clerisy and probably have the same origin. Lay-offs have hit the overclass, the class to which many professors and media people belong, and from which these people typically draw their friends. Increasingly, households in the upper fifth of incomes comprise two professionals or managers, and while professionals and managers were more immune to lay-offs than blue-collar workers twenty years ago, that no longer holds. Now, to repeat, given that professionals and managers are pairing off two-by-two in greater and greater numbers, overclass families have far more reason to be anxious than they did twenty years ago. The debt load of such people is often staggering, and the loss of one job can mean foreclosure.

Still, Nisbet would not cry too hard for these overclass households, households wherein the ancient family virtues of honor, duty, and obligation have sometimes been replaced by the utilitarian calculus and simple greed (TA, 256-257; PA, 88-89). Certainly dual-earner households are typically not due to economic necessity. Dual-earner families make 70 percent more than single-earner intact families, a gap that has grown over time; and married women are more likely to work, the higher their husband's income.[52] The trend toward dual-earner families, like the increase in single-parent households, has contributed to the shrinkage of the American middle class, but it also elevates the class standing of certain households. Increasingly, the rich in the United States are dual-earner families; the median income for these families is at the eightieth percentile for all families. Nonetheless, the widening gap between single-earner and dual-earner families has not restrained the overclass's support of their interest. Overclass families, for example, often invoke "collective responsibility" and agitate for federalized day care. They hope one day to see state power become Nanny. What advocates fail to mention, of course, is that a federal day care program would require taxing the lower middle class—traditional, single-earner families—in order to subsidize the often debt-ridden, gaudy lifestyles of the overclass. Indeed, such a program would entail an increase in taxes such that thousands—perhaps hundreds of thousands—of current stay-at-home mothers would be compelled to enter the labor force. As Nisbet regularly observes, such are the typical effects of state power employed to "help" families (see 1962, xii-xiii; TA, 80-85).

The principal reason for the widening gap between intact single-earner and dual-earner families is the decline in male wages since the early 1970s.[53] Bellah et al. note that many households have responded to this by sending a second family member into the labor force. What they fail to note, however, is that in addition to being an effect of the decline in male wages, the increase in women who work is a cause of this decline because of the increased competition for jobs. It is also *the chief cause* of the increased age of marriage, the decline in marriage and birth rates, and the higher divorce rates over the last forty years.[54] Nisbet observes that "millions of young women and young men are discovering that the old, now obsolete, worker-homemaker partnership between husband and wife was a sturdy foundation of many interpersonal relationships which today are difficult to create" (PA, 121).

Doubtless, Bellah and his co-authors are silent regarding these problems because acknowledging the consequences of female workers would require criticizing what Nisbet in *Twilight of Authority* calls, potentially "the most fundamental of modern social movements"—feminism. Nisbet says this because feminist ideology "is directed at the most ancient roles in human history: those of the two sexes" (82). Certainly, no recent social movement has been as important as feminism in valuating market participation as the highest source of one's identity and in denigrating the private and intimate sphere. The transcendent ends of the "puritan ethic" have been replaced by base and avaricious ends; and the "feminist ethic" has replaced the puritan ethic as capitalism's most important ideological prop.

In addition to the competition of women, the competition for jobs that has suppressed male wages has come from the sheer numbers of baby boom workers, from high school students, the majority of whom work during the school year (compared with 5 percent working in 1950); and from the millions of new American immigrants during the past thirty-five years. No doubt more than all this is involved in the decline in male wages, but just as certainly Bellah et al. greatly mislead their readers on this count by focusing exclusively on the globalization of the economy and on the dwindling union membership "stemming from legislative changes in the last twenty years."[55] Regarding the latter, union membership, as Bellah et al. note, peaked in "the middle 1950s." What the authors fail to say, however, is that it declined as much or more between 1958 and 1976 (a period in which real male wages increased by over 50 percent) than since 1976.[58] The causes of this decline are not legislative. As Nisbet asserts, the decline of the unions is more likely due to "politicization" (PA, 75).

Monistic and Pluralistic Solutions

Bellah and his co-authors afford an almost pristine example of contemporary political monism. The sources of American problems for Bellah et al., as we have seen, are structural. They lie with the "large structures" of the economy and state, and to get at these sources, we are told, requires a form of "republicanism or nationalism," the center of which is "national consensus and national action."[56] Individuals must "seek the common good."[57] In this view, to focus on the family or on face-to-face communities is "sadly mistaken" because "the deep structural problems" of our society cannot be alleviated with so narrow a focus.[58] Our problems are rooted in "failures of collective responsibility."[59] Indeed, the health of smaller communities depends ultimately "upon the well-being of the whole."[60] Accordingly, Bellah and his co-authors call us "to wider and wider circles of loyalty ultimately embracing that universal community of all beings...."[61] Such loyalty is the essence of what the authors call "civic membership." Civic membership ennobles the individual while leading to the betterment of society.[62] As things are, our "civic life is a shambles." Our "crisis in civic membership" has depleted our "social capital" and even threatens our personal identity.[63]

Following Robert Putnum, the authors define "social capital" as "features of social organization, such as networks, norms and trust, that facilitate coordination and cooperation for mutual benefits."[64] The two most important indices of social capital are associational memberships and trust in public institutions, both of which, the authors claim, have declined in recent years for "structural reasons," especially those stemming from "changes in the economy."[65] Similarly, personal identity is threatened because it "is conferred primarily by one's relationship to the economy, by one's work and the income derived from one's work."[66]

I suppose Putnum and Bellah et al. can define terms in any way they want. Nonetheless, their conception of "social capital" differs greatly from the idea as originally developed by Glenn Loury and James Coleman, and the original idea—now employed by many social scientists—is a much more useful concept.[67] It is quite simply *Nisbetian* in that it is explicitly not directly concerned with economic and political structures or with extended notions of community. Specifically, Loury and Coleman define social capital as "the set of resources that inhere in family relations and in community social organization and that are useful for the cognitive and social development of a child or young person."[68]

For Loury and Coleman, social capital concerns the resources provided by those with whom someone has face-to-face contact, especially family, and personal identity is a matter of the character developed before entering the adult world of work—although these resources and this identity ultimately affect adult behavior.

In addition to the theoretical grounds provided by Nisbet, the empirical grounds for preferring this conception of social capital to that of Bellah et al. should be clear enough at this point. The causes of American problems, including the decline in our social capital, are just as Tocqueville imagined them a century and a half ago and as Nisbet has described them over the course of his half-century career. As Tocqueville put it, there are "three great influences which regulate and direct American democracy"—physical causes, laws, and mores—"but if they are classed in order, I should say that the contribution of physical causes is less than that of the laws, and that of the laws less than mores."[69]

By "physical causes" Tocqueville meant the influence of geography, but his point is preserved if this term is taken to mean economic or material causes. Each of these three "great influences" has its effects in America today and Tocqueville's order of importance remains the same. The evidence suggests that material causes are real but not as significant as laws and mores. Laws are important but less important than our manners and morals. Our mores, our customary beliefs and practices, mold us most directly and most powerfully. They, in fact, largely mold and shape our laws as well. For example, our no-fault divorce laws have contributed to our high divorce rates, but these laws conform to our current mores. Indeed, as noted, Nisbet maintained that "the alleged disorganization of the modern family is, in fact, simply an erosion of its natural authority, the consequence, in considerable part, of the absorption of its functions by other bodies, chiefly the state" (1962, xii). As Nisbet argues, though, this is often less a matter of the aggressive advance of power than of the willing retreat of authority. Ideas, morals, and customary beliefs are the vital forces in history (TA, 233), and it is mainly what beats in our hearts that is at the source of our problems. In a word, our problems are primarily "cultural" in origin.

Nisbet observes that, without "a clear sense of cultural purpose, membership, status and continuity…no amount of mere material welfare will serve to arrest the developing sense of alienation in our society, and the mounting preoccupation with the imperatives of community" (QC, 73). Regarding the current state of our culture, Nisbet is an excellent guide. His first observation today would no doubt be to point out the clear indications that we are turning the corner, that we are beginning to reconstitute our social order in beneficial ways. But he would also acknowledge how far we have to go in order to revive our culture. Our culture has failed to domesticate males, the results of which are as they have everywhere been—violence. Our culture has replaced the natural purpose of marriage, the rearing of children to maturity, by the emotional and sexual gratification of adults; a gendered division of labor has given way to an androgynous ideal buoyed by avarice; we have somehow convinced ourselves of a woman's exclusive right to choose, but we are perplexed to find that men often refuse to shoulder responsibility for what they are told are women's choices. Our culture hopes for paternal investment but erodes the confidence of men. It is a culture in which marriage is deemed a mere contract and volitional fatherlessness has become routine. Our manners and morals have led to laws by which shucking one's spouse and children is easier than firing an employee, and violators of the marital covenant suffer fewer consequences than someone who breaches a business contract. Ours is "an age of cultural sterility, of 'failure of nerve,' of philosophical morbidity" (QC, 235). Most concretely, our culture, as Nisbet maintains, is one in which individuals are separated and estranged from the authority and hierarchy of genuine communities, the contexts that form of true character.

Bellah and other statist communitarians such as Charles Taylor and Michael Walzer cannot comprehend these circumstances because, like most contemporary liberals, they eschew tradition and the bonds of customary communities. Indeed, as Bruce Frohnen has recently argued in *The New Communitarians and the Crisis of Modern Liberalism*, the "new" or statist communitarians and contemporary liberals are not opposed to one another, for they are equally committed to individual autonomy. "Communitarians do not seek to replace liberalism," Frohnen asserts, "but to save it. Providing liberalism with an understanding of man's social nature and needs, communitarians hope to reinvigorate liberal society."[70] But, as Bellah's writings reveal, the new communitarians have a politicized view of society. They "seek to convince us that democratic politics is the source of moral rules and values." They decry the belief that "individuals can govern themselves without the aid of a tutelary state—a government that teaches virtue."[71] For the new communitarians, the true community is the national community, and the virtues to which they enjoin others are political virtues—tolerance, equality, universal benevolence, social justice, and nondiscrimination.

Despite the writings of Bellah and other contemporary statist communitarians, there is no *effective* opposition to the public institutions of free markets and limited government *as such* in America. Nonetheless, America's ostensible liberal society has, through subtle, moderate, and mixed ways, departed quite dramatically from the Founders' vision. The traditional liberal public order is a formal mechanism that requires a people of a particular character: a people who resist immediate gratification, whose natural social sentiments are formed in a home free of political intrusion, who undertake their civic duties, and who would follow and yield to the approbation and disapprobation of their peers. Put bluntly, a bourgeois public order requires a bourgeois people, but although the requirements of the bourgeois ethos are far from demanding, such an ethos is clearly weakening.

In the spirit of Nisbet, we might call our prevailing ethos "hypertrophic liberalism," a pervasive everyday ethos which, like statist communitarianism, rests upon a confusion of what is appropriate to the private and public realms (PA, xi; TA, vii). Hypertrophic liberalism, however, is something of the reverse—yet complementary—image of statist communitarianism: the two are not opposites but mutually sustaining poles, each of which is opposed to the distinction between realms necessary for genuine ordered liberty. Where statist communitarianism is the inappropriate extension of communal principles to the public realm, hypertrophic liberalism is the extension of public order principles to natural communal settings. Hypertrophic liberalism sponsors what we can call "spurious contractualism," the misapplication of contractual thinking, so basic to a proper conception of the economy and government, to relations in the private realm. Thus, Americans typically see marriages not as a source of natural obligation, but as a mere contract between consenting adults. Similarly, hypertrophic liberalism promotes "radicalized tolerance," a form of tolerance flung well beyond the public realm, where it is salutary, to the private realm, where it is often mere indifference to the evil that individuals do to themselves and to others. And finally this ethic fosters the "universal benevolence" about which Burke and Smith wrote and which, according to both men, is associated with particularistic indifference. All considered, in their different yet complementary ways, both statist communitarianism and hypertrophic liberalism ignore the intermediate communities that are essential to human well-being, and together they are rendering our communal or socializing institutions incapable of discharging their chief function of fashioning souls.

The family is, of course, the most important social institution. As Nisbet says, "It is the family, not the individual, that is the real molecule of society, the key link of the social chain of being" (TA, 260). He goes on to say, "The great contributions of kinship to society are, on the one hand, the sense of membership in and continuity of the social order, generation after generation; and on the other, the spur to individual achievement, in all areas, that the intimacy of the family alone seems able to effect" (TA, 253). In fact, he notes, "Almost certainly it is the form and significance of the family tie rather than racial or genetic stock that explains individual achievement in history" (TA, 255). Variations in the family tie, also note, account for variation in group achievement as well. Those groups in America that have low divorce and illegitimacy rates—Jews and Asians, for example—outperform other groups in educational achievement and are at the top of the income heap. Regarding the latter, Jews and American-born Asians have household incomes 50 percent higher than white gentiles.[72]

To revive the American family would require restoring its authority and functions (TA, 252-260). Doing so would be a very important step in rejuvenating social life; but, according to Nisbet, it would be far from sufficient. For the family to perform its vital functions, the church, the school, the local community, and voluntary associations must all be aligned in mutual support. Consequently, in concluding both *The Quest for Community* and *Twilight of Authority*, Nisbet describes the need to rehabilitate, or create, a plurality of communities in order to rejuvenate American life (also see SED, 136-145). At the center of his suggestions is what he calls a "new laissez-faire," a "form of laissez-faire that has for its object, not the abstract individual, whether economic or political man, but rather the social group or association" (TA, 276). This new laissez-faire would not replace the old one but supplement it. "The liberal values of autonomy and freedom of personal choice are indispensable to a genuinely free society, but we shall achieve and maintain these," Nisbet says, "by vesting them in the conditions in which liberal democracy will thrive—diversity of culture, plurality of association, and the division of authority" (QC, 279). We need to create conditions wherein autonomous groups can prosper.

The single largest obstacle to creating such conditions, Nisbet says, is the political clerisy vested in the idea of "national community" and in the schemes for state improvement. Nonetheless, he asserts the historical record is a source of hope because "just as twilight ages are a recurrent phenomenon in Western history, so are ages of social replenishment, of reinvigoration of social roots." The Middle Ages, for example, were rich in social inventions. "Monastery (in its distinctive Western form), village community, manor, fief, guild, university, parish: these are some of the notable inventions—'developments' as we are more likely to say—of the medieval period." Similarly, a great richness existed in the seventeenth century "with its creation of institutes and academies in the arts, letters and sciences, all admirable as means of uniting the creative impulses of individuals in the areas represented." And, more recently, the nineteenth century responded to the democratic and industrial revolutions with "mutual aid in new forms, the consumers' and producers' cooperatives, assurance societies, the labor unions, and the business corporations...." The history of social organization, he suggests, "comes down basically to the history of the rise and spread of social inventions—relationships among individuals which, once found useful and accepted, have in many cases gone on for thousands of years in a variety of civilizations" (TA, 280-281).

Intermediate association and social invention are the stuff of history, according to Nisbet, because we are naturally animated by a "social impulse," the "impulse to form associations of whatever kind in which significant function or role in the larger society can be combined with the sense of the social bond, of social authority, that is so fundamental to freedom in any of its significant forms" (TA, 276). Releasing this impulse from the restraints imposed by government and by the attitude of mind supported

by the intellectual mandarinate would inevitably promote association, invention, and even indirect administration. Thus, for
example, educational vouchers would provide the household
with indirect administration of education, as well as the opportunity for social invention and voluntary association. Vouchers,
Nisbet believes, would stimulate the creation of new schools that
could not treat parents and students as passive clients. Indeed,
such a scheme would promote "citizenship" in the original sense
of the term. Originally, a person was a "citizen" by virtue of free
association in the town or city (TA, 279-287).

Our circumstance, according to Nisbet, should inspire action, not despair. Indeed, as Francis Fukuyama has documented,
recent signs indicate that such actions are being undertaken
and that we are beginning to address the problems brought on
by the "great disruption" of the last forty years.[73] Still, much
needs to be done and large obstacles remain. Chief among these
are the ideas and influence of materialists and monists. The
appeal of views such as Bellah's is tremendous. They externalize
problems and their solutions. What *we* believe and how *we* behave in our everyday lives have nothing to do with the causes of
problems such as "cancerous individualism," illegitimacy, educational deficiencies, income inequality, and domestic violence,
for these are conveniently attributed by materialists to external
conditions. We are mere marionettes. Similarly, what *we* believe
and how *we* behave are irrelevant to solutions, because other

people, politicians, captains of industry, and the like—the pup-
peteers, if you will—are the only ones capable of effecting change
in the all-important external, material conditions. At least part
of the appeal of deterministic explanations is that they ask so
little of those who espouse them.

Nisbet, by contrast, believes that intermediate association,
indirect administration, and social invention require that *we*
act. We must inspect our hearts, our mores. In his view, all
effective change begins with our salient beliefs, manners, and
morals. Clearly, Nisbet's worldview is at a great disadvantage in
the marketplace of ideas. But it has the more than minor advantage of being *truthful.* For those who are serious about the truths
of our social world and who seek guidance on how to better it,
his works are an excellent place to start.

NOTES

Introduction

1. Quoted by Maurice Natanson in the editor's introduction to Alfred Schutz, *Collected Works* vol. 1 (The Hague: Martinus Nijhoff, 1962), xxv.

2. Nicholas Lemann, "Paradigm Lost," *The Washington Monthly* 23 (April, 1991), 46. For evidence of Nisbet's impression upon the New Left, see C. George Benello, "Participatory Democracy and the Dilemma of Change," in Priscilla Long, ed., *The New Left: A Collection of Essays* (Boston: Porter Sargent, 1969). Paul Goodman and the authors of the Port Huron Statement claimed influence from Nisbet.

3. Michael Sandel, *Democracy's Discontent* (Cambridge: Harvard University Press, 1996); Alan Ehrenhalt, *The Lost City* (Chicago: University of Chicago Press, 1995); Amitai Etzioni, *The Spirit of Community* (New York: Crown, 1993); Don Eberly, *America's Promise: Civil Society and the Renewal of American Culture* (Lanham MD: Rowman and Littlefield, 1998); Francis Fukuyama, *Trust* (New York: Free Press, 1995); Robert Putnum, "Bowling Alone: America's Declining Social Capital," *Journal of Democracy* 6 (1995) 65-78; Peter Berger and Richard John Neuhaus, *To Empower the People* (Washington, D.C.: American Enterprise Institute, 1996). Of these authors, only Don Eberly and Berger and Neuhaus acknowledge Nisbet's genius, although Ehrenhalt argues persuasively the Nisbetian view that community depends upon authority and that valorizing individual choice destroys community.

Chapter 2

1. Herbert Spencer, *The Man Versus the State* (Indianapolis: Liberty Press, 1982).

2. David Hume, *An Inquiry Concerning the Principles of Morals* (Indianapolis: Bobbs Merrill, 1957), 20.

3. David Hume, *Essays: Moral, Political and Literary* (Indianapolis: Liberty Press, 1985), 39-40.

4. Alexis de Tocqueville, *Democracy in America* vol. II trans. Henry Reeve (New York: Vintage, 1990), 300-301.

5. Alexis de Tocqueville, *The Old Regime and the Family Revolution* trans. Stuart Gilbert (New York: Anchor, 1955), 208.

6. Joseph Schumpeter, *Capitalism, Socialism and Democracy* (New York: Harper and Row, 1942), 160.

7. See Philip Rieff, *The Triumph of the Therapeutic* (New York: Harper and Row, 1966); *Fellow Teachers* (Harper and Row, 1972). Rieff is a spirit kindred to Nisbet and a much neglected thinker. In *Fellow Teachers,* he discusses education and he describes the easy melding of money and the therapeutic. Symbolic of this melding is the Nietzscheanized use of the term "value" in therapeutic discussions of moral matters. As Rieff observes, "When I hear the term 'value,' I reach for my wallet; the word should be left to the barkers of schlock on the mass media, giving good 'value' for your money. 'Value' is a word which should only be used for purpose of marketing spoilt goods "(7).

Chapter 3

1. Richard Weaver, *Ideas Have Consequences* (Chicago: University of Chicago Press, 1948).

2. Karl Popper, *The Open Society and Its Enemies* (Princeton: Princeton University Press, 1950).

3. Aristotle, *The Politics* trans. Carnes Lord (Chicago: University of Chicago Press, 1984), 1261a1 15-35, 1261b1 17-41; 1262b1 14-24.

4. Thomas Hobbes, *Leviathan* (New York: Penguin, 1968), 120.

5. Ibid., 161.

6. Ibid., 185.

7. Ibid., 186. It can also be noted that although John Rawls speaks in *A Theory of Justice* (Cambridge, Mass.: Harvard University Press, 1971) of "the original position" and "the veil of ignorance," instead of the natural

condition, his methodology mirrors Hobbes's. Like Hobbes, Rawls manages to remove all considerations of ascribed and historically constituted sources of authority from his political philosophy. The family, for example, is not treated in Rawls's discussion of the original position. Within this theoretical enterprise, all authority is political authority and the end of political society is justice conceived as equality. Nisbet is very critical of Rawls (TA, 214-219); as he observes, "inequality is the essence of the social bond" (TA, 217).

8. John Locke, *Second Treatise of Government* (Indianapolis: Hackett, 1980) par. 93.

9. Hobbes, *Leviathan*, 223.

10. Ibid., 254.

11. Ibid., 373.

12. Ibid., 374.

13. Ibid., 375.

14. Ibid., 285.

15. Jean-Jacques Rousseau, *Emile* trans. Allan Bloom (New York: Basic Books, 1978), 213.

16. Ibid., 92.

17. Ibid., 214.

18. Jean-Jacques Rousseau, "The Disclosure on Inequality," in *The Basic Political Writings of Jean-Jacques Rousseau* trans. Donald Cress (Indianapolis: Hackett, 1987), 55.

19. Ibid., 60.

20. Ibid., 65.

21. Ibid., 67.

22. Ibid., 93.

23. Ibid.

24. Jean-Jacques Rousseau, "The Discourse on the Sciences and the Arts" in *Basic Political Writings*, 7.

25. Allan Bloom, "Rousseau—The Turning Point," in *Confronting the Constitution* ed. Allan Bloom, (Washington, D.C.: AEI Press, 1990), 214.

26. Ibid.

27. Ibid., 212.

28. Jean-Jacques Rousseau, "The Social Contract," in *Basic Political Writings*, 163.

29. Pierre Manent, *An Intellectual History of Liberalism* trans. Rebecca Balinski (Princeton: Princeton University Press), 77.

30. Jean-Jacques Rousseau, *"The Social Contract,"* 223.
31. Ibid.
32. Ibid., 226.
33. Ibid.
34. Ibid., 222-223.
35. Edmund Burke, *Further Reflections on the Revolution in France* (Indianapolis: Liberty Press, 1992), 48-50.
36. Edmund Burke, *Reflections on the Revolution in France* (New York: Anchor, 1989) 22, 187, 242.
37. Burke, *Further Reflections*, 47.
38. Ibid., 169.
39. Burke, *Reflections*, 263.
40. Ibid.
41. Ibid., 213.
42. Ibid.
43. Ibid., 59.
44. Ibid., 110.
45. Ibid., 213.
46. Ibid., 101.
47. Burke, *Further Reflections*, 49.
48. Burke, *Reflections*, 228-229.
49. Tocqueville, *Democracy*, 318.

Chapter 4

1. Louis Hartz, *The Liberal Tradition in America* (New York: Harcourt, Brace and World, 1955).
2. In *Natural Right and History* (Chicago: University of Chicago Press, 1950), Leo Strauss describes Burke's view with references to another principle, one from which Darwin drew inspiration. Strauss observes, "the sound political order for [Burke], in the last, is the unintended outcome of accidental causation. He applied to the production of sound political order what political economy had taught about production of public prosperity...." (314-315). Strauss is referring, of course, to the Smithian principle that individuals can unintentionally promote the public good by pursuing their private interests. It should also be noted that Strauss believed that the Burkean historical school unknowingly contributed to historicism, relativism, and the view that human nature does not exist, "that man's humanity

[is] acquired by virtue of accidental causation" (315). The latter view Strauss associates with Rousseau. This is not the place to take up this controversy beyond noting my deep suspicion of any viewpoint from which Burke and Rousseau appear kindred spirits.

3. Quoted in Sissela Bok, "From Part to Whole" in Joshua Cohen ed. *For Love of Country* (Boston: Beacon Press, 1996), 43.

4. Isaiah Berlin, *Four Essays on Liberty* (Oxford: Oxford University Press, 1969), 127.

5. Ibid., 132.

6. Ibid., 156. Brief reflection on John Gray's *Isaiah Berlin* (Princeton: Princeton University Press, 1996) provides insight into Nisbet's thought. Gray characterizes Berlin as an "objective pluralist" because, on the one hand, Berlin insisted against moral relativists that reason is capable of discriminating between good and evil practices, and, on the other hand, he insisted against monists that there exists a plurality of genuine and morally salutary practices (46-47). Gray also calls Berlin an agonistic liberal, "taking the expression from the Greek word *agon*, the meaning of which covers both competition or rivalry and the conflict of characters in tragic drama" (1). According to Berlin, although reason provides a standard by which to judge between moral and evil practices, it cannot provide a standard by which we can choose among different moral practices. "Berlin's agonistic liberalism...grounds itself on the radical choices among incommensurables, not upon rational choice" (8). Given that Nisbet abjures moral relativism and that he also doubts the existence of a divine or natural standard that will allow us to rank communities and moral practices, there are clear and profound similarities between Berlin and Nisbet. Certainly, the terms "objective pluralist" and "agonistic liberal" apply as well to Nisbet as to Berlin.

7. In Nisbet's discussion of conservative dogmatics, he separates "Liberty and Equality" from "Property and Life." In my brief account, I combine them under the heading "Liberty and Equality."

8. Tocqueville, *Democracy*, 146.

Chapter 5

1. Plato, *The Laws* trans. Thomas Pangle (New York: Basic, 1980), 681d, 678d.

2. Richard Gill, *Posterity Lost: Progress, Ideology, and the Decline of the American Family* (Lanham, Md.: Rowman & Littlefield, 1997).

Chapter 6

1. There is one intriguing exception to this neglect. In *The Making of Modern Society*, Nisbet briefly describes Montesquieu as a pluralist and in a single sentence he refers to Locke and Hume as social pluralists, linking the latter names to those of Burke and Tocqueville (25, 28-29).

2. Typically today when the distinction between private and public is made, the private realm is portrayed as the place of individuals and their interests, while the public realm is portrayed as a social realm. This inverts the classical liberal distinction and conveys one of the means by which statists or political monists have transformed terms to suit their political ends. Revolutions do indeed begin with the dictionary. The essential texts of classical liberalism are: Locke, *Second Treatise*; Montesquieu, *The Spirit of the Laws* trans. Anne Cohen, Basia Miller, and Harold Stone (Cambridge: Cambridge University Press, 1989); David Hume, *A Treatise of Human Nature* (Oxford: Clarendon Press, 1978) and *An Inquiry Concerning the Principles of Morals* (Indianapolis: Bobbs-Merrill, 1957); Adam Ferguson, *An Essay on the History of Civil Society* (New Brunswick, N. J.: Transaction Press, 1980); Adam Smith, *An Inquiry into the Nature and Causes of the Wealth of Nations* (Indianapolis: Liberty Press, 1981) and *The Theory of Moral Sentiments* (Indianapolis: Liberty Press, 1982).

3. Hume, *Essays*, 259.

4. Hume, *Principles*, 24-25.

5. Montesquieu, *Spirit of the Laws*, 154-168.

6. Ibid., 17-19.

7. Smith, *Wealth of Nations*, 606.

8. Smith, *Wealth of Nations*, 26-27

9. Smith, *Wealth of Nations*, 788-814.

10. Hume, *Treatise*, 316-324; Adam Smith, *Moral Sentiments*, 9-178.

11. Smith, *Moral Sentiments*, 113.

12. Ibid., 111-112. See Hume, *Treatise*, 303, 365. Also compare with Charles Cooley's famous discussion of the looking-glass self in *Human Nature and Social Order* (New York: Scribners, 1902), 184. Nisbet (SB, 60) cites Cooley when discussing the "looking-glass self."

13. Arthur Lovejoy, *Reflections on Human Nature* (Baltimore: The John Hopkins Press, 1961), 129-215.

14. Smith, *Moral Sentiments*, 219-227.

15. Ibid., 235-237.

16. See Charles Cooley, *Social Organization* (New York: Scribners, 1909), 25-50; Franklin Giddings, *The Principles of Sociology* (New York: Macmillan, 1896); William Sumner, *Folkways* (Boston: Ginn, 1906).

17. Quoted in Ian Ross, *The Life of Adam Smith* (Oxford: Clarendon, 1995), 181; and Conor Cruise O'Brien, *The Great Melody* (Chicago: University of Chicago Press, 1992), 144.

18. Quoted in Ross, *Adam Smith*, 355.

19. Burke, *Further Reflections*, 198-199. I should note as well that of Locke, Burke said, "The authority of this great man is doubtless as great as that of any man can be...." See Burke, *On the Sublime and Beautiful* (New York: P. F. Collier and Son, 1909), 114.

20. Robert Bellah, Richard Madsen, William Sullivan, Ann Swidler, and Steven Tipton, *Habits of the Heart*, updated edition (Berkeley: University of California Press, 1996), xiii. Hereafter HH. Bellah's Rousseauianism is evident in virtually everything he has written. It is most explicit, however, in his writings on civil religion. See "Civil Religion in America," in *Beyond Belief* (New York: Harper and Row, 1970); "The Revolution and the Civil Religion," in *Religion and the American Revolution*, edited by Jerald C. Brauer (Philadelphia: Fortress Press, 1976).

21. Robert Reich, *The Work of Nations* (New York: Knopf, 1991); and Michael Lind, *The Next American Nation* (New York: Free Press, 1995).

22. HH, xiv.

23. Christopher Jencks, *Rethinking Social Policy* (New York: Harper, 1992), 76; and Lawrence Mead, *The New Politics of Poverty* (New York: Basic Books, 1992), 31.

24. Francis Fukuyama *The Great Disruption* (New York: The Free Press, 1999), 44.

25. Ibid., 32, 42. Accounting for the recent declines in violent crime is of course a difficult matter. My own sense is that these declines are attributable chiefly to community policing and to the incarceration of violent criminals. Economic factors have perhaps also had an effect. Nonetheless, even with a very low current unemployment rate and an eight-year economic expansion, violent crime rates are much higher today than in 1960. Also, it can be noted that the period between 1960 and 1973 saw a 260 percent increase in violent crime rates, although this was a very prosperous time. Some of this increase—perhaps 20 percent—can be attributed to demographic factors, but what remains of this increase can not be accounted for in terms of "structural factors."

26. For the comparisons of black and white incomes, see Bureau of the Census, Table F-7, *http//www.census.gov/hhes/income/histinc/f07.html*. For the effects of fatherlessness on income, see Sara McLanahan and Gary Sandefur, *Growing Up with a Single Parent* (Cambridge: Harvard University Press, 1994).

27. Sylvia Ann Hewlett, *When the Bough Breaks* (New York: Basic Books, 1991), 92.

28. James Collier, *The Rise of Selfishness in America* (New York: Oxford University Press, 1991), 255.

29. Barbara Defoe Whitehead, "Dan Quayle Was Right," *Atlantic* (April, 1993), 77; and David Popenoe, *Life Without Father* (New York: Free Press, 1996), 63.

30. David Blankenhorn, *Fatherless America* (New York: Basic books, 1995), 55-56.

31. Ibid., 35. Blankenhorn estimates that only 9 percent of all male domestic violence (including the violence of boys) is committed by husbands. Another Justice Department report estimates that 29 percent of adult male domestic violence is committed by husbands. See David Popenoe, *Life Without Father*, 73-74. Popenoe, 64-73, also discusses the increases in the physical and sexual abuse of children attributable to the increased numbers of single-parent households, live-in boyfriends, and step-parents. Such abuse is rare in households with both biological parents but common in these other contexts.

32. William Julius Wilson, *The Truly Disadvantaged* (Chicago: University of Chicago Press, 1987). In his most recent book, *When Work Disappears* (New York: Knopf, 1996), Wilson recognizes the independent and important influence of culture. Wilson is an honest scholar. Nonetheless, his main focus remains on economic conditions as the cause of social pathologies.

33. A third of out-of-wedlock births are to middle-class women, a fact for which Wilson cannot account. See Blankenhorn, *Fatherless*, 81.

34. Lawrence Mead, *New Politics*, 99-109.

35. Ibid.

36. Ibid., 76-84.

37. Andrew Cherlin, *Marriage, Divorce and Remarriage* (Cambridge: Harvard University Press), 104-105.

38. HH, xii.

39. HH, xiv.

40. HH, xxvii.

41. William Bennett, *The De-Valuing of America* (New York: Summit, 1992), 55.

42. This relationship can be analyzed using numerous sources. See, for example, Marion Cetron and Margaret Gayle, *Educational Renaissance* (New York: St. Martin's Press, 1991), 240-325.

43. Gary Orfield and Carole Ashkinaze, *The Closing Door* (Chicago: University of Chicago Press, 1991), 140-141.

44. Regarding the characterological virtues, a summary is provided by William Donohue, *The New Freedom* (New Brunswick, N.J.: Transaction Press, 1990), 168-169. The studies of one-parent and two-parent children are discussed in Daniel Patrick Moynihan, *Family and Nation* (San Diego: Harcourt Brace Jovanovich, 1986), 92-93.

45. HH, xv.

46. William Julius Wilson, *Truly Disadvantaged*, 10.

47. Andrew Cherlin, *Marriage*, 92. See National Center for Children in Poverty, *Five Million Children* (New York: Columbia University Press, 1992), 29, for the study of children in persistent poverty. The Census Bureau findings are discussed in Ben Wattenberg, *Values Matter Most* (New York: The Free Press, 1995), 93-95.

48. HH, xv.

49. HH, xv.

50. HH, vii.

51. HH, viii..

52. The 70 percent figure comes from the Census Bureau, Table F-7, *http://www.census.gov/hhes/income/histinc/f07.html*. According to F. Carolyn Graglia in *Domestic Tranquility* (Dallas: Spence Publishing, 1998), 74, "In 1988 only 42 percent of women with husbands whose income fell below the median worked, as opposed to 71 percent of those whose husbands earned more than the median."

53. HH, xxxii.

54. Andrew Cherlin, *Marriage*, 52. For a discussion of the effects of female labor force participation on both men and women, see Graglia, *Domestic Tranquility*, and Lionel Tiger, *The Decline of Males* (New York: Golden Books, 1999).

55. HH, xx. The figures on high school students who work come from Laurence Steinberg, *Beyond the Classroom* (New York: Simon and Schuster, 1996), 164-182.

56. HH, xxviii.

57. HH, xxix.

58. HH, xxii-xxiii.

59. HH, xxiii.

60. HH, xxix.

61. HH, xxx.

62. HH, xxxi.

63. HH, xxxviii, xxxi.

64. HH, xvi.

65. HH, xvii. Also see Putnum, "Bowling Alone." Everett Ladd in *The Ladd Report* (New York: Free Press, 1999) has taken issue with Putnum's claims concerning the decline in associational memberships. Indeed, he demonstrates that if anything, such memberships have recently increased. I believe that this points to the superiority of James Coleman's definition of social capital, given its emphasis on children and socializing institutions. It also suggests that to address social pathologies, a rehabilitation of the family is needed. Voluntary associations are beneficial mainly when they are adjuncts to the family, church, and other institutional agents of childhood socialization.

66. HH, xviii-xix.

67. See, for example, McLanahan and Sandefur, *Growing Up with a Single Parent*.

68. James Coleman, *Foundations of Social Theory* (Cambridge: Harvard University Press, 1990), 300. Coleman is quoting Loury.

69. Alexis de Tocqueville, *Democracy in America* vols. I and II trans. George Lawrence (New York: Anchor, 1969), 308.

70. Bruce Frohnen, *The New Communitarians and the Crisis of Modern Liberalism* (Lawrence, Kans.: University Press of Kansas, 1997), 22.

71. Ibid., 24.

72. See Christopher Jencks, *Rethinking Social Policy* (New York: Basic Books, 1992), 28; and Lawrence Harrison, *Who Prospers?* (New York: Basic Books, 1992), 165.

73. Fukuyama, *The Great Disruption*.

INDEX